THE GREAT CROSSING

THE GREAT CROSSING

A Historic Journey
to Buffalo Trace Distillery

RICHARD TAYLOR

BUFFALO TRACE DISTILLERY

ISBN 0-971683-70-0 (paper edition)

ISBN 0-971683–1-9 (cloth edition)

LCCN 2002-100079

Contents

[ILLUSTRATIONS FOLLOW PAGE 56]

Special thanks to

John Gray of Historic Frankfort, Inc.,

Neal O. Hammon, and the Kentucky Historical Society

for securing the use of the selected illustrations and photographs.

Acknowledgments

There are a number of people whose help has been indispensable in producing this book. I am grateful to the Hay family — E. H. Taylor Hay, Jr., John Hay, and Mary Belle Harwich for information and family stories about their forebear E. H. Taylor, Jr. Likewise, Mrs. V. O. "Jinks" Barnard, another descendant of Colonel Taylor, provided useful stories as well as an abundance of genealogical information about the Taylor family. Alice Blanton and her nephew Robert Howell, Jr., related facts about the Blanton family's long association with the distilleries at Leestown. Ron Bryant of the Kentucky Historical Society, Charles Hockensmith of the Kentucky Heritage Council, Jonelle "Jo" Fisher of Midway, and my good friend Neal O. Hammon of Shelbyville all graciously offered material and insights that filled in gaps that helped keep the manuscript and me on track. And thanks to John Gray of Historic Frankfort, Inc. and the Kentucky Historical Society for securing the use of selected illustrations and photographs.

Most especially, I want to acknowledge the work of D. G. Churchill in his unpublished "Ancient Age Through the Ages: The Whiskey History of Leestown, Kentucky, 1769-1982." His comprehensive history of distilling at Leestown was a key source in the preparation of this book, and, though I have never met him personally, I am indebted to him for his painstaking and insightful study of the whiskey tradition at Leestown.

Finally, I want to thank Chris McCrory and Mark Brown at Buffalo Trace Distillery as well as Kim Aubrey of Black Sheep, Inc., for giving me the opportunity to explore the history of an industry that is so indigenous and central to the economic and social history of Kentucky. Their support and encouragement at every stage of the writing are much appreciated. Thanks also to Lizz, my wife, who is always on hand to guide me through the intricacies of computer technology.

RICHARD TAYLOR, MAY 28, 2001

I.

"A Richer and More Beautiful Country..."

IMAGINE A RIBBON OF GREEN winding through a river valley, flanked by wooded slopes that rise from an extensive flood plain. Close by the water is a sandy beach and shelves of limestone through which the currents work miniscule but steady etchings along the embankments, a process that began long before a species existed that could witness and record it other than through their own fossilized remains embedded in the rock itself. Above the beach is a band of brushy vegetation, a shrubby growth of river birch, and silver maples dwarfed by overhanging sycamores and other water-loving trees. The level of the "beechy bottom" is also timbered with oaks and poplars, giving way on the plateau to oak, sugar trees, walnuts, ash, locusts, hickories, and buckeyes — a green canopy that stretches as far as the eye can see in a succession of timbered ridges. In places there are thick brakes of cane whose jointed stalks and spear-shaped leaves rustle and shush in the breeze that comes off the water. Near the narrow beach where the water riffles are shoals that form a natural ford. And on each shore is a trail about a hundred feet wide with dust several inches deep. The surface is pocked with funnel-shaped indentations from thousands of hooves, but there are no wheel ruts, not a single footprint. As the trail cuts to the water, it forms a groove or trough worn over the centuries by the friction of scuffing hooves. Along the well-trod trail and in patches of natural meadowland is a rich variety of bluegrass, white clover, pea vines, and buffalo grass that is high as a man's waist. Nowhere in this landscape is there a straight line or any other sign of measured symmetry. Nowhere is there evidence of humans — no structures, no felled trees, no cultivated ground. On the eve of the American Revolution in the third quarter of the eighteenth century, all of this was to change both rapidly and irrevocably.

On May 24, 1775, a party of nine men set up a camp at the ford on the flats along the sandbar. Exhausted after another day of paddling their dugout canoes up the Kentucky, they had lashed them together in the shallows, eating from their meager store of bread and the remaining fillets of a buffalo heifer shot the day before. Bone-tired, they had turned in at nightfall. For fear of attracting hostile Indians, they doused their small cooking fire and simply rolled up in their blankets on the beach. The two servants who accompanied the party usually made their beds in the canoes, but this night fortunately elected to sleep on shore instead. Only one man, Benjamin Johnston, who had come to take up land in Kentucky, chose to sleep in a canoe, the one closest to shore.

Sometime during the night the campers were alarmed by a commotion in the river, a thrashing in the water. When Johnston shouted for help, the others, anticipating an Indian attack, grabbed their arms and rushed to the dugouts. They found one of them half-submerged, the remainder of their precious supply of flour almost totally destroyed. The damaged canoe would have sunk entirely had it not been attached to the other, which luckily remained afloat. They dragged the wooden pod and its soggy contents to shore, then tried to sort out what had happened.

Johnston told them that he awakened to find himself among a drove of buffaloes that were crossing the river. They had jumped over the canoe in which he was sleeping and crushed the second canoe, splitting it along the greater part of its length. The servants, it was clear, would have been killed had they been resting in their customary places. Though much of the next day was spent laboriously caulking the damaged canoe with bark of the white elm and installing knees between the weakened gunwales, they counted themselves lucky.

The party was headed by Nicholas Cresswell (1750-1804), a young English traveler from Derbyshire who kept an elaborate diary of his adventures in the New World, an account that his descendants released for publication nearly one hundred and fifty years later. Two days before the buffalo incident, Cresswell and his party had been paddling up the Kentucky River in two canoes. In a show of youthful bravado he had named them the Charming Polly and the Charming Sally. As the party made its way toward its next stopping place at what became Leestown, Cresswell noted "several rapids which obliged us to get out and haul our vessel up with ropes." He and his companions had camped the night before on a hill in a "beech thicket" where "all hands" were "well tired and D—d cross."

Among the party whose destination was the rude camp at what was to become Fort Harrod were James Nourse (another Englishman who also kept a journal), Benjamin Johnston, George Rice, brothers Edmund and Reuben Taylor, and two indentured servants. Part of the way they were accompanied by Captain George Rogers Clark. Because everyone was in "great fear" of the Indians, Cresswell had put out two scouts to walk on either side of the river, the rest to work the canoes upriver and relieve each other by turns. The weather was rainy, and the going along the river was especially hard on the scouts who clambered over gullies and waded among weeds as high as a man's head. During the day Cresswell had noted seeing several buffalo tracks and a flock of "Paroquets."

Buffaloes in the wilds of Kentucky were not the only obstacles to be overcome. On May 29 the company "proceeded a little way up the River to a great Buffalo crossing," where the liberty men quarreled with Cresswell about politics. Loyal to his king, Cresswell defended the Crown against the verbal attacks of Edmund Taylor — the elder of the Taylor brothers — and several of the others, whom Cresswell described as "red-hot liberty men." In another confrontation Cresswell records that one of his "discourses" on politics ended in "high words" and Edmund Taylor's threat to tar and feather him. A willing subject of King George III among those whose allegiance was doubtful, Cresswell and his traveling companions alike would soon hear "the shot heard round the world" at Concord Bridge, news of which would give a campsite twenty-five miles to the east its identity as a settlement. Tensions must have been high because Cresswell reports that George Rice, a partisan for independence, threatened "to scalp and tomahawk" him. Mutual fear of a more immediate threat of marauding Indians must have, temporarily at least, united the parties in some form of rough civility.

As they approached the rapids, Cresswell "saw several roads that crossed the River which they tell me are made by the Buffaloes going from one lick to another." "These licks," he noted, "are brackish or salt springs which the Buffaloes are fond of." He estimated that his party had traveled twenty miles that day with no sign of Indians. The next day, as they made their way upriver against a strong current and more rapids, the party "surrounded" thirty buffaloes as they were crossing the river. They "shot two young Heifers and caught two calves alive whose ears we marked and turned them out again." They were nearing the future site of Leestown where the "great buffalo road," one of the most important trails in the Ohio River Valley, crossed the Kentucky River.

Cresswell's diary gives one of the earliest and fullest descriptions of the area around Leestown. His entry on May 24 contains notations about the landscape that he could observe from his canoe: "Land in general covered with Beech. Limestone in large flags. Few rivulets empty into the River, or few springs to be seen."[1] His account of the buffalo incident also conveys the sense of danger, not all of it from Indians, that many of the earliest settlers must have felt as they traveled deeper into the Kentucky country. The place where they met with near disaster "where the Buffaloes cross the river" would become the site of one of the earliest distilleries in Kentucky:

In the night [we] were alarmed with a plunging in the River. In a little time Mr. Johnston (who slept on board) called out for help.

We ran to his assistance with our arms and to our great mortification and surprise found one of our Canoes that had all our flour on board sunk, and would have been inevitably lost, had it not been fixed to the other. We immediately hauled our shattered vessel to the shore and landed our things, tho' greatly damaged. It was done by the Buffaloes crossing the River from that side where the vessel was moored. Fortunately for Mr. Johnston he slept in that Canoe next the shore. The Buffaloes jumped over him into the other, and split it about fourteen foot.[2]

On May 30, James Nourse, Rice, and Taylor went "to take a view of the country," and Cresswell records his own response to the landscape in the vicinity:

Mr. Johnston and I took a walk about 3 miles from the river, find [*sic*] the land pretty level, a blackish sandy soil. Timber chiefly beech. In our absence those at the Camp caught a large Catfish which measured six inches between the eyes. We supposed it would weigh 40 pounds.[3]

Returning from his own trek the next day, Nourse described the land a distance from the river as "the levelest, richest and finest they ever saw, but badly watered."[4]

The pathway that James Nourse had been following from the river was known to the Indians as Alant-o-wamiowee, the Great Buffalo Trace. It passed from the river through the uplands of Franklin County and eastward toward what are now Fayette and Scott Counties. Described as one of the important buffalo "roads" in the Ohio Valley, it followed a southerly course up the west side of the Kentucky River from Drennon's Lick in what is now Henry County. At Leestown, near the site of present-day Buffalo Trace Distillery, it crossed the river at a natural ford (one of the few on the entire river) near the mouth of a stream now called Cove Spring

Branch and passed up a "Great sand beech" to higher ground through what is the heart of the distillery grounds. At that time — before the building of locks, which raised and controlled water levels — the river during most of the year consisted of a series of riffles and pools.

The unsettled country into which Cresswell traveled during the summer of 1775 was claimed by Virginia. Because Virginia owed its allegiance to Great Britain at the time, the area north and east of the Kentucky River, including Leestown, was referred to by the earliest pioneers and explorers as "Crown lands." From the viewpoint of Native Americans the country belonged to all of them in common and constituted an enormous game reserve that existed for their sole benefit.

They deeply resented the incursions of white and black Americans, whom they regarded as interlopers. Since Eskippakithiki ("the place of the blue licks"), the last remaining permanent Indian town, had largely been abandoned in the 1750s, the Kentucky country was no longer permanently inhabited by Indian peoples, serving instead as a huge hunting ground, to which no one group or individual had exclusive rights.

Looking east on what is now Holmes Street in Frankfort, one can still spy a gap in the high bluffs. This break in the ridgeline forms a natural passage through which the buffalo passed to what is now East Frankfort and generally in an easterly direction toward Lexington or Stamping Ground and Great Crossing in Scott County. At Stamping Ground hundreds of buffalo gathered at the lick to extract the salt so necessary to their diets. Stamping Ground got its name "from the fact that the animals in vast herds would tread or stamp the earth while crowded together and moving around in the effort of those on the outside to get inside and thus secure protection from the flies."[5] Great Crossing, two miles west of Georgetown, marks the place where the herds crossed North Elkhorn Creek on their journey toward the salt lick.

From there, the trail continued along an eastward course to Blue Licks, May's Lick, and across the river into the Ohio country. In some places the buffaloes cut paths with six-foot-high banks, and in others the trail was wide enough for two wagons to pass each other. As demonstrated by Cincinnati,

Louisville, Lexington, and Frankfort, these roads in large part dictated not only lines of travel and transportation established by migrating buffalo but where settlements and cities would form.

For hundreds of years before the first Euro-Americans saw this buffalo trail, it attracted aboriginal hunters, who recognized the spot as ideally suited for hunting buffalo, elk, and white-tailed deer. At the ford where Alant-o-wamiowee crossed the Kentucky, great herds traversed the water on their way to the salt springs at Stamping Ground, Great Crossing, and Royal Springs (at Georgetown) toward what is now Paris, Kentucky, on the South Fork of Licking River. These trails later formed the routes for Kentucky's first network of roads, including Leestown Road between Leestown and Lexington, one of the earliest in central Kentucky and demarcated on John Filson's 1784 map of the Kentucky country.

On the west side of the river the buffalo trail extended northwest along the west side of the Kentucky River toward Drennon Springs in Henry County, then across the river to Big Bone Lick where the bones of prehistoric mammoths and other extinct mammals were preserved in the saline muck. Both sides of the river derived names from the presence of buffalo. On the west side, the area of Franklin County known as Bald Knob was named for the droves of buffalo that grazed the hilly uplands in their ceaseless foraging. Another fork of the buffalo trail continued west from Leestown up Big Benson Creek to Shelby County and the Falls of the Ohio at Louisville, roughly following what is now US 60. Though less true today, the river valley then was an early "hub" of travel, owing then to its accessibility to the river at a point that was fordable at most times during the year.

The first white man known to record his impressions of the area is explorer and surveyor Christopher Gist (c. 1705-1759), a pioneer woodsman who passed through the Leestown/Frankfort river bottom in 1750. Gist was commissioned by a group of Virginia and English landowners calling themselves the Ohio Company. His mission was to survey an enormous tract of land granted them by King George II. Starting in late October 1750, Gist and a "young black companion" (probably the first recorded man of color to visit this region) navigated down the Ohio nearly to the Falls, then traveled in a southerly direction through Kentucky and southeastern Virginia, returning to the Yadkin Valley of North Carolina in November 1751. While in Kentucky, Gist traveled to Blue Licks and Drennon's Lick. He then followed Alant-o-Wamiowee through what is now eastern Shelby County to Big Benson Creek and the Kentucky River area near Frankfort before continuing southeast through present Woodford and Fayette Counties to the border of Clark. Though spare and matter-of-fact, his journal entry is the earliest recorded visit to the area:

> Tuesday, March 19, 1751, We set out south and crossed several creeks all running to the southwest, at about 12 M. came to the …Cuttaway (Kentucky) river; We were obliged to go up it about 1 m. to an island which was the shoalest place We could find to cross at. [mouth of Benson Creek] We continued our course in all about 30 m. through level rich land which was broken and indifferent. This level is about 35 m. broad.…

In the fall of 1752, John Finley (1748-1837), the early Indian trader who first described the wonders of the Kentucky country to Daniel Boone, passed through the Leestown area but left no record of the experience. Nearly two decades later, during the summer of 1770, Boone himself traveled through the same area, making his way from the Falls of the Ohio to his camp in southern Clark County. As he came to the river along the buffalo road, he spotted an Indian fishing from the trunk of a fallen tree. Boone was alone. The Indians had robbed him and his companions of their horses and pelts, killing his friend John Stewart. As his son Nathan reported years later, Boone, a Quaker, never directly acknowledged shooting the fisherman but would simply say, "While I was looking at him, he tumbled into the river and I saw no more of him." In his comings and goings through the Kentucky country Boone passed through the Leestown area many times. Other than mentioning his untimely meeting with the fisherman, he did not later comment on these visits.

In the spring of 1773, three brothers — James, George, and Robert McAfee of Augusta County, Virginia — left Virginia and came down the Kanawha and Ohio Rivers in dugout canoes to explore Kentucky. Accompanied by Matthew Bracken and Samuel Adams, they journeyed down the New and Kanawha Rivers, then joined surveyors Thomas Bullitt and Hancock Taylor (1738-1774), who were also on their way to the Kentucky country in search of desirable land. Splitting off from Bullitt and his surveying party, they descended the Ohio and canoed up the Kentucky twenty-one miles to Drennon's Creek where they found the river "shut up by a stone bar." From there they proceeded overland, following the Indian trail to the great buffalo crossing at Leestown. They described the buffalo road, which was 100 feet wide, and noted that its dust was several inches deep and that hooves over time had worn the ground level down several feet to form a kind of groove. Thousands of buffalo had crossed the river for hundreds of years in their search through the Bluegrass for salt. To give some idea of the scale of the road as it passed through the "gap" into the uplands beyond Leestown, the trestle that the Frankfort and Cincinnati Railroad Company later built over the buffalo trace was 156 feet high and 800 feet long.

The formation of the river valley east and north of what is now Frankfort suggests that the Kentucky River ran to the east and north of Fort Hill (down Holmes Street) in place of being on the west side where it currently runs. The valley which begins at the head of Holmes Street at the site of the old penitentiary opens out onto the river again below Lock 4 near Leestown. Much of the bottomland that constitutes Frankfort and Leestown is situated on what geologists describe as a deserted meander of the Kentucky River. Most of low-lying Frankfort had at one time or another been the channel of the Kentucky, one of the oldest rivers in eastern North America.

Assisted by Hancock Taylor, the party made a number of surveys in the wide bottom that now comprises the city of Frankfort. Returning to Virginia along the Indian trail through Pound Gap (and nearly starving), the McAfees later came back and established one of the first settlements

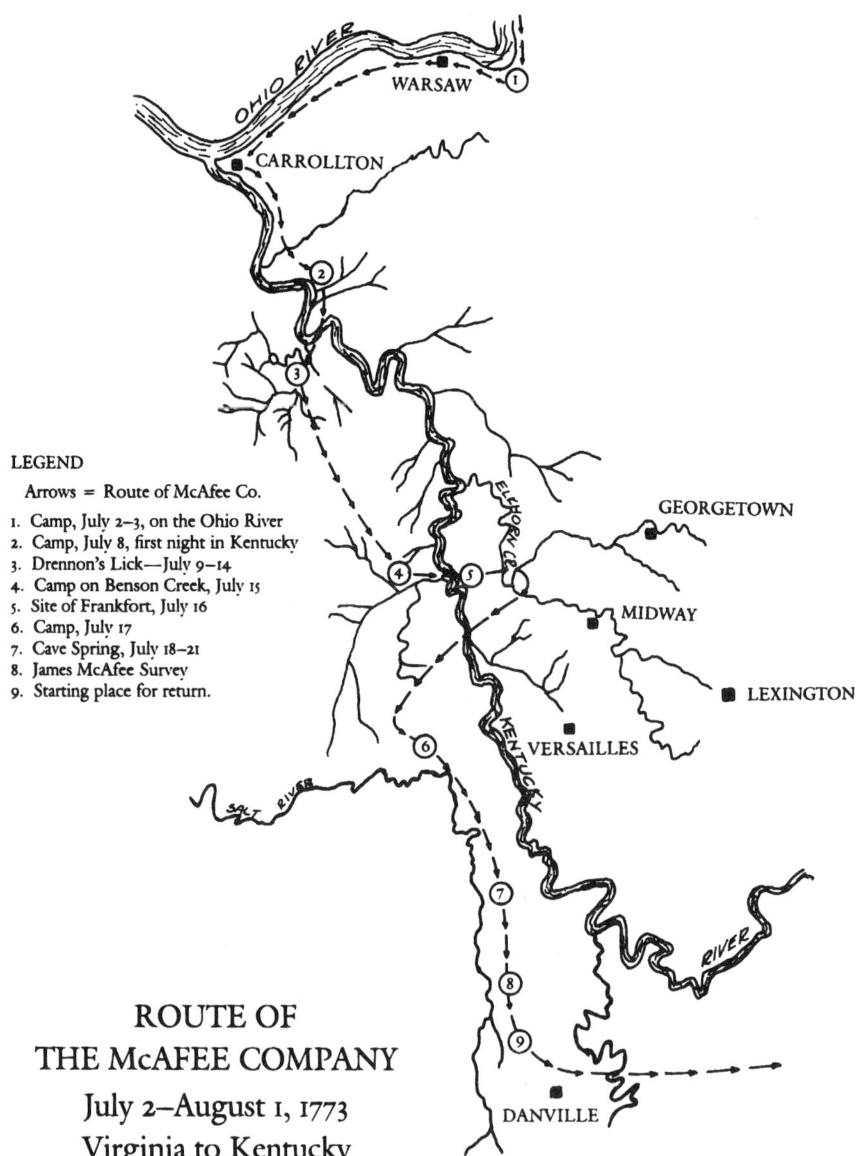

OHIO RIVER
WARSAW
CARROLLTON
ELKHORN CR.
GEORGETOWN
MIDWAY
LEXINGTON
VERSAILLES
KENTUCKY
SALT RIVER
RIVER
DANVILLE
LEGEND
Arrows = Route of McAfee Co.
1. Camp, July 2–3, on the Ohio River
2. Camp, July 8, first night in Kentucky
3. Drennon's Lick—July 9–14
4. Camp on Benson Creek, July 15
5. Site of Frankfort, July 16
6. Camp, July 17
7. Cave Spring, July 18–21
8. James McAfee Survey
9. Starting place for return.
ROUTE OF
THE McAFEE COMPANY
July 2–August 1, 1773
Virginia to Kentucky

on Salt River in what is now Mercer County. After the larger party split up, Lee, Taylor, and his assistant Abraham Hapstonstall journeyed to the Falls of the Ohio from which they made their separate way back to Virginia.

Hancock Taylor was the first of a number of Taylors, all originating from Orange County, Virginia, who were to have associations with the Leestown area. Trained as a surveyor in a family of land-hungry planters, Taylor already had extensive experience "upon the western waters." In 1769 he, his brother Richard (father of President Zachary Taylor), and one companion canoed down the Ohio to its confluence with the Mississippi and then downriver to New Orleans. His companions traveled home by land, but Hancock voyaged by ship to New York and made his way to Virginia after a two-year journey.

Surveyors Taylor, Thomas Bullitt, Willis Lee, John Floyd, and others, including the McAfees, were drawn to Kentucky when Virginia's western-most county was opened to veterans of the French and Indian War. Starting on July 16, 1773, Taylor ran surveys for the McAfees in the Lees-town area, the first made in the river bottom where Leestown and Frankfort formed and among the first in Central Kentucky. Much of Robert McAfee's survey encompassed the grounds of the Buffalo Trace Distillery (though the property came into other hands when he settled farther upriver and permitted his claim to lapse).

Because many of these initial surveys were not officially recognized by William Preston, chief surveyor of Fincastle County, Taylor returned to the Bluegrass the next year to make additional surveys as part of an authorized surveying party. On June 17, 1774, he surveyed two hundred acres for his father Zachary Taylor (the future president's grandfather) "by virtue of the Governor's Warrant and agreeable to his Majestie's [*sic*] Proclamation…of 1763, on a branch of the Kentucky which empties at the great crossing." This description confirms that the ford at the mouth of Cove Spring, known also as Leestown Branch, was the site of an extensive buffalo crossing point. The claim was adjacent to Robert McAfee's. On May 12, 1780, Hancock Lee entered 500 acres on a Treasury Warrant, "be-ginning at Zachariah Taylor's corner, near McAfee's spring branch, in a bottom known by the name of Lee's Town, and to run down the branch to the mouth."[7]

During the summer of 1774, Daniel Boone and a young wilderness scout named Michael Stoner were sent to the Kentucky country to warn settlers of a major outbreak of Indian hostilities. Traveling hundreds of miles in a matter of days, they were too late to save Hancock Taylor and one of his companions, ambushed on July 17 while they paddled up the Kentucky. Mortally wounded, Taylor was able at first to walk and survived for some days before finally dying in Madison County on August 1. His cousin Willis Lee buried him in an unmarked grave on what is now called the Taylor Fork of Silver Creek. During the summer he had made twenty-nine individual surveys in the Bluegrass, an amount that totaled 47,250 acres.

Willis Lee was with Taylor at the time of his death. Taylor and his one surviving companion Abraham Haptonstall had managed to rejoin the main surveying party before his death. Willis Lee, named as a beneficiary and an executor under Taylor's will, dated July 29, 1774, took charge of Taylor's effects — his books, papers, field notes, and the will itself. He carried them back to Virginia and duly recorded them. Within a year some of his heirs and beneficiaries came to Leestown in pursuit of their land interests.[9]

Hancock Taylor's earlier companion, Robert McAfee, who later settled near Harrodsburg in Mercer County, recorded his impressions of the Leestown area when he visited in 1773:

> Thursday, the 15th [July 1773], took a small buffalo path which was about 50 and a hundred yards wide in common about 30 miles across low flat ridges, middling good land and timber but no water. The 16th we went about 6 miles and came to the same river — Cantuck — and crossed it to the sunrise side, and then 2 miles across to another bend. The land on the river seemed to be very full of beech; and from that point I made two surveys, near joining to the river, with about 50 acres of meadow now ready made, and there can be made 50 acres more with a little

trouble; with bottom and upland sufficient, with very good water in different places of it.[10]

The "path" he describes is the great buffalo trail at Leestown.

His brother James McAfee, who also kept a journal, has a parallel entry during this time:

> The 15th of July [1773] we left the Great Salt Lick, took a path to the right of the river up a creek [Drennon's] a south course of about 30 miles and camped that night. The 16th. In five miles we cross the Century [Kentucky] River to the east side along the path; fives miles in a piece of black old oak timberland; we stopped and survey(ed?) one tract of land for Robert McAfee containing 600 acres, about 100 of that meadow ground. Friday 16th, left an axe, tomahawk, and fish gig at the [McAfee] springs.[11]

James McAfee elsewhere described Robert's survey as being situated "at the great meadow" on the river.

Robert McAfee's claim, located about a half-mile from present-day Cedar Cove Springs, later supplied Frankfort with water run through bored cedar pipes that functioned effectively until 1886. As early as 1804, Richard Throckmorton started laying a water line from the spring to serve Frankfort, a distance of three miles. The waters of Cove Spring (also called Cedar Cove Spring) provided a sufficient quantity to serve as the source for the first municipal water system in Kentucky and one of the earliest in the West.

When James Nourse, Edmund Taylor, and George Rice temporarily left their companions in the Cresswell party on May 30, 1775, they started from the "paved landing along a buffalo path." According to historian Neal Hammon, who reconstructed the courses of the buffalo roads from both Nourse's journal and existing landmarks, the path that the buffalo appeared to follow was from Leestown Landing (the site of the distillery) "around the north side of Fort Hill, then across the existing stone quarry, and climbing the hill in the ravine behind this quarry to the plateau of

East Frankfort, then to a point on the west side of Black's Pond…." [This is today's Silverlake Subdivision on US 460.][12]

Nourse describes their coming "to the foot of a steep hill or mountain over which the path led — steep and rocky but not so bad but a horse might now go up and is capable of being made a wagon road — it is about two miles from the river on the top of the hill." Reaching the top of the hill, he noted that the land was "light with timber, consisting of little oak— mostly sugar tree, Walnut, Ash, and buckeye. I call horse chestnut, but the tops of the trees mostly scraggy. The surface of the ground [is] covered with grass along the path which was as well trod as a market-town path for about twelve mile." The ground cover was a mixture of bluegrass, white clover, buffalo grass and reed pines "and waist high what would be call[ed a] fine swarth of grass in cultivated meadows, and such was its appearance with-out end in little dells."[13] Along the way they sighted five herds of buffalo and killed a calf for dinner.

Cresswell's journal gives one of the earliest surviving topographical reports of the Central Bluegrass. He described the land a distance from the river as the "levelest, richest, and finest they ever saw, but badly watered."[14] After rejoining Nourse, the next morning they all headed upriver toward "Harwood's Landing" [that is, Harrod's Landing on the Kentucky].

Though several of the the area's visitors mention the terrain at the point of crossing, it is the Englishman Cresswell who embodied most fully what he saw in the Leestown area. Note, for example, his eye for detail in portraying the buffaloes he encountered along the river:

> Buffaloes are a sort of wild cattle, but have a large hump on the top of their shoulders all black, and their necks and shoulders covered with long shaggy hair with large bunches of hair grow-ing on their fore thighs, shorts horns bending forward, short noses, piercing eyes and beard like a goat.[15]

He goes on to cite their penchant for salt and their road-making abilities:

They are fond of Salt or Brackish water. Springs of this sort have
large roads made to them, as large as most public roads in a
populous country. They eat great quantities of a sort of reddish
Clay found near Brackish springs.[16]

On June 11, Cresswell discovered the party of Hancock Lee a short distance downriver. They were camped at Elkhorn Creek busily surveying
sites in the vicinity. The next day Cresswell was welcomed at Lee's camp:

Went to Captn. Lee's camp, who treated me very kindly with a
dram of Whiskey and some bread, which at this time is a great
luxury with me. Captn. Lee's brother gave me a Rattlesnake about
four feet long. Very hot.[17]

Lee, like Hancock Taylor, was a deputy surveyor under Colonel William
Preston, the chief surveyor of Fincastle County, Virginia. Lee, who succeeded George Washington as chief surveyor for the Ohio Company,
founded Leestown to promote his company's interest in the Kentucky
country. He was probably in the vicinity of Leestown on information
conveyed by his brother Willis and cousin Hancock Taylor, who had first
visited the area with the McAfee brothers during the summer of 1773. The
best estimate is that Lee and his party arrived at the mouth of Elkhorn
Creek about June 1, 1775, and went on to the site of Leestown about two
weeks later. On December 7 Hancock Lee "entered" 400 acres with Colonel
Preston. Lee's 400 acres was located "upon the North side of Kentucky
River, including a large spring, it being the head of the run (or branch)
that empties in at the sand beech [*sic*] at Lees Town."

As historian Samuel Wilson describes it, the rich bottomland at Leestown was ideally situated either for a "headquarters" camp or a permanent
settlement:

Lying in a sharp bend of the river, near a shallow ford of shelving
rock, and with a spacious sandy beach on which to land and load

or unload canoes and other boats, and with never-failing springs
of cold, pure water near at hand, with a large natural meadow in
easy reach and a rich bottom of level land sufficiently extensive
to provide the settlers with an abundant supply of corn, and
with broad buffalo roads radiating to the East and West, it is by
no means surprising that this particular spot had attracted the
eye of Robert McAfee and Hancock Taylor and was afterwards
chosen by Hancock Lee as the site for his town.[18]

And — one might add — a distillery.

Finding the spot so much to their liking that they made other survey entries in the vicinity, Hancock and his brother Willis proceeded to lay out Leestown, the second-oldest settlement to be established on the Kentucky River and the oldest in the Commonwealth north of the river. On another claim nearby they planted a field in corn by the "great Buflow road." The Lee claims in and around Leestown were distributed among Richard, Hancock, Henry, and Willis Lee. Located at a sharp bend in the river near a shallow ford of shelving rock, their holdings extended nearly a mile in every direction. The broad, sandy beach was convenient for the loading and unloading of canoes or other vessels, the cold-running spring for a reliable source of fresh water, the meadow land for planting corn, the buffalo roads radiating east and west affording a ready means for land travel and transport. Though the Lees made claims elsewhere, they showed an obvious preference for the Leestown area, citing the spring and crossing place as key topographical features.[19] The convergence of buffalo trails also placed Leestown, located about a mile below Frankfort at what was to become Lock No. 4, strategically along what later became the Louisville-Lexington Road.

The Lees originally came to Kentucky as agents of the Ohio Company, a land company projected in 1748 by Thomas Lee of Westmoreland County, Virginia, a man with political connections who for a time served as Virginia's acting governor. The original grant to the company included 500,000 acres, and its broad purpose was to settle families, build a fort for their protection, and maintain a garrison for defense. Having originally employed Christopher Gist to identify and survey likely lands in the western country, it recruited its agents from the best Virginia families, of whom the Lees are representative. During its existence of over forty years, the company never prospered, largely due to competing companies and supervening events, namely the French and Indian War (which awarded land to Virginia veterans) and the Revolution, which extinguished it.

According to records in Fincastle County, Virginia, for December 27 1775, Hancock Lee took the necessary legal steps to enter the Lee claims for acreage, property that would become the core of their claims at Leestown. Following customary procedures, he "produced memorandums," entering 400 acres on the north side of the Kentucky River "including a large spring being at the head of a run that empties at the sand beach at Lees Town." He entered two claims of 400 acres joining this claim and 400 acres at the "Great Buffalow crossing on Cedar Creek" as well as 400 acres on Rich Land Creek "at a mulberry tree" and 400 more joining this claim. Downstream at the mouth of Elkhorn Creek on the north side of the river he had two claims of 400 each. His total was 2,800 acres, the largest parcel (1,200 acres) at Leestown.

Richard Lee entered 800 acres, 400 of which were located about a mile downstream from the "great sand beach" on a "Great Buflow Road" joining an entry of Willis Lee. Willis himself claimed 2,800 acres, some above and some below Leestown. One claim was located on the north side of the Kentucky River opposite the mouth of Benson's creek and included a large beaver pond. Another was two miles below Leestown on the Great "Bufflow Road" to "include the corn field planted by Hancock Lee." Richard Lee entered 800 acres in the vicinity and Henry Lee 1,600 acres, one portion of which was "on the lower side of Elkhorn" about a mile from the mouth to include a cabin built by Willis Lee. What these entries show, in addition to an inability to decide on a consistent spelling of "buffalo," is a sizeable quantity of land claimed by the Lees (8,800 acres), most of it concentrated at Leestown and to a lesser extent downriver in the vicinity of Elkhorn Creek.[20]

The founding of Leestown followed the settlement at Fort Boonesborough by only two months or so. Richard Henderson, the proprietary founder of Boonesborough, was early quite familiar with his neighbors downriver. In his July 20, 1775 journal entry in what he calls his "Expedition to Caintuckey," Henderson mentions that Captain Linn and his company had set off to "Lee's settlem[ent] with whom I sent two men for a little salt."

The first settlement in what is now Franklin County, Leestown at the time of its formation was a part of Fincastle County, Virginia. Before the end of 1776, Virginia made it a part of Kentucky County, later subdividing Kentucky County into Lincoln, Jefferson, and Fayette. The Leestown area became a part of Fayette County, from which Franklin County was later portioned off. As one of the likeliest crossing points on the river, it became a favorite stopping place for early settlers, travelers, surveyors, and hunters. It was to become a commercial center for the transport of goods downriver.

Writing about the Leestown settlement of 1776, Humphrey Marshall describes it as "a place of general rendezvous for hunters and improvers." Significantly, he mentions that several cabins were built there "but not in the order of a fort."[21] He also notes that there were some other cabins on the same side of the river (the north side), "but of inferior note." He goes on to offer an explanation for the abandonment of the area: "Not being able to withstand the attacks of the Indians, the whole settlement after Willis Lee's death were [*sic*] broken up, and abandoned."[22]

During the winter of 1780-1781 the surveyor and pioneer settler Colonel John Floyd (1751-1783) took advantage of the cabins at Leestown, either those that remained after the attack in 1776 or those that had been built and abandoned afterwards. His unannounced plan was to lay up meat for General George Rogers Clark's projected expedition to take British forts in the Northwest Territory. In a letter to Clark, dated April 16, 1781, Floyd mentioned the ill-fated hunting venture he organized at Leestown:

I have been more unfortunate in my little hunt last winter

[1780-1781] than the rest. I hired seven or eight men, went to Lees [*sic*] cabins with horses loaded with salt, gave 1000 [pounds] for building canoes; killed & saved 54 buffaloe, 4 elk & 2 large wild hogs & brought it safe to between Goose Creek & Beargrass [on the Ohio six miles from the Falls] where my vessells were overset by a gale of wind and sunk my whole cargo to the bottom. Besides the meat tallow &c, I lost five guns, my saddle bags, surveying affairs, warrants, field books & all memorandums about land for seven years past, and as the people saying in their advertisements, many other articles too tedious to mention. This is my second defeat at sea, but I am alive and hearty.[23]

Floyd had been captured by the British earlier in the war and taken to England, where a judge acquitted him of any wrongdoing. After a series of adventures he had made his way back to the western country. Educated, enterprising, Floyd unfortunately, like his fellow surveyors Hancock Taylor and Willis Lee, lost his life to the Indians. A veteran who served George Rogers Clark on his expeditions against the Shawnee in Ohio, Floyd died April 10, 1783, two months after the war had officially ended, of wounds suffered in an Indian ambush near the Salt River. He was reportedly buried in the scarlet cloak he was wearing at the time of the ambush.

Other adventurers and travelers soon made their way to the ford at the Leestown settlement. When geographer Jedidiah Morse came to the area in March 1789, he ignored Frankfort, probably because it was only a "paper town." Morse mentioned that Leestown "is regularly laid out and is flourishing."[24] He also noted that topography contributed to the success of the site:

The banks of the Kentucky River are remarkably high, in some places 300 and 400 feet, composed generally of stupendous perpendicular rock. The consequence is there are few crossing places; the best is at Leestown, which is a circumstance that must contribute to its increase.[25]

Lee's hospitable gesture to Cresswell, mentioned earlier, was appropriate to a site that was to be identified with distilling, the more so because the royalist Cresswell and he were politically at cross purposes. Nevertheless, Lee hospitably greeted him with the offer of whiskey: "Went to Captn. Lee's camp, who treated me very kindly with a dram of Whiskey and some bread, which at this time is a great luxury with me."[26]

The desolateness of Kentucky before settlement tended to draw travelers together. Cresswell's next notation underscored the wildness of the place. After refreshing Cresswell, Lee's brother Willis showed Cresswell a specimen of the local wildlife — the skin of a four-foot-long rattlesnake. Planting what was probably the first crop of corn in the area during that summer, Lee laid the groundwork for what was soon to become a thriving whiskey industry.

A month later, George Rogers Clark, then serving as deputy surveyor for Hancock Lee and assisting Lee in laying out the town, wrote an enthusiastic letter to his brother Jonathan Clark:

> … A richer and more beautiful country than this I believe has never been seen in America. I am engrossing all ye land I possibly can.… We have laid out a town seventy miles up ye Kentucke where I intend to live, and I don't doubt that there will be fifty families living in it by Christmas.[27]

Clark himself soon went on upriver to Fort Harrod. Events during the next few years prevented him from making good his intention and delayed others as he led Virginia's war in the west during the Revolution that broke out the next year.

About the first of June, 1775, Willis and Hancock Lee of Fauquier County, a branch of the Virginia Lee family so prominent in Virginia and American history, arrived at the mouth of Elkhorn Creek and set up a camp. Employed by the Ohio Company, which had been formed to promote the financial interests of its proprietors in land speculation, they had traveled up the Kentucky River, arriving about the middle of June at the great crossing and future site of Leestown. Hancock Lee knew of this place from his brother Willis, who had accompanied Hancock Taylor on both of his surveying forays into the Kentucky country during the summers of 1773 and 1774.

Recognizing the commercial value of the site as a practical point at which to load and unload goods, Hancock soon laid out the town, starting at the buffalo crossing by the river. Its assets were obvious: the river, a sandy beach, the nearby spring, and the generous stretch of bottom land along a river where access was often a problem. Leestown lay in a picturesque river valley surrounded by towering hills whose timbered slopes and ridge-lines extended indefinitely over the countryside.

But the location north of the Kentucky River also made Leestown more vulnerable, and the first fatality at Leestown was its founder. In April 1776, Hancock's brother Willis was killed by Indians when they attacked and burned several cabins at Leestown. Cyrus McCracken, another defender, was wounded but escaped with the others. The sole fatality, Lee was mortally wounded and left near the blockhouse door by the survivors, who, fearing for their lives, fled to Boonesborough. Evidently, the defenders tried to make him comfortable because when travelers Daniel Campbell and Robert Edmiston, having come up the Kentucky River by canoe, found him a short time later, he was dead, "a pail of water sitting by his head, his hands lying on his breast, and the blood coming up through his fingers."[28] Vulnerable because of its location and its fluctuating population at any given time, the settlement often had to be abandoned under threat of Indian attack.

The attack on Leestown in 1776 was said to have been carried out by a party of Mingoes, an independent band of Iroquois-speaking Indians who were allies of the Shawnee and lived in western Pennsylvania and western Virginia near the headwaters of the Ohio. Their famous chief, Logan, had begun a war of retaliation in 1774 after a mob of whites murdered members of his family. It is also likely that the deaths of surveyor Hancock Taylor and his companion James Strother were consequences of the agitation caused by these same murders.

Not long after, in June 1776, some Mingoes captured the twin sons of Alexander McConnell only a hundred yards or so from the Leestown settlement. McConnell, a Pennsylvanian, had migrated to Leestown during the preceding winter, planted a crop of corn, and built a cabin. During the next winter he sent for his family. On a summer day in June, Mrs. McConnell sent an indentured boy and her two sons, Adam and William, to bring in their cows to be milked. They were set upon by a small party, who killed the servant and captured one of the twins while the other hid. Seeing his brother's distress, the other twin surrendered. When the twins reached the Shawnee towns north of the Ohio on the Scioto River, they were recognized by Joseph Nicholson, who knew their father. After some negotiation, he was able to exchange them for a rifle. Through the efforts of Col. George Morgan, an agent of Congress visiting the Indian town where they were taken, the twins were not forced to run the gauntlet. With the added aid of "King" Cornstalk, Morgan secured their release and accompanied them to Pittsburgh, where they joined their uncle William McConnell, who lived in nearby Westmoreland County. They were in the hands of the Indians about sixty days. As an unhappy postscript, their father Alexander McConnell was killed in northern Kentucky at the Battle of Blue Licks in 1782, the so-called last battle of the American Revolution.[29]

In a letter to Col. William Preston dated July 21, 1776, surveyor John Floyd, describing the condition of the Kentucky settlements from Boonesborough, refers to the Indian troubles at Leestown:

> The situation of our country is much altered.... The Indians seem determined to break up our settlements, and I really doubt, unless it was possible to give us some assistance, that the greatest part of the people must fall a prey to them. They have, I am satisfied, killed several. Many are missing who, some time ago, went out about their business who we can hear nothing of. Fresh sign of Indians is seen every day. I think I mentioned to you before, some damage they had done at Leestown.[30]

In an earlier letter to Preston dated May 21, Floyd refers to Hancock Lee's death but unfortunately gives only sparse details: "I need say nothing about the mischief which has been done, as Mr. [Hancock] Lee, brother to Willis Lee who is killed, can give you a history of the whole that may be relied on."[31]

Describing Leestown during this period in his "Narrative" written in 1791, General Levi Todd of Fayette County confirms that Leestown was abandoned for a time:

> Leestown is now uninhabited. It is on the north side of the Kentucky river about 23 miles N. 10 [degrees] west of Lexington and about two miles below Frankfort. This fall a great part of the adventurers returned to the Settlements, some to bring out their families, some for farming utensils, some for their commissions and a great many to spread the names of the American canaan, but all to get fresh rigged with clothing.[32]

Leestown is the oldest "thriving" settlement on the Kentucky River. Its slightly older sister to the southeast, Boonesborough, though preserved today as a state park with a replica of the original fort, ceased to exist as a community long ago. Willard Rouse Jillson describes Leestown as "the first surveyed and fortified settlement north of the Kentucky River." Lewis and Richard Collins briefly described the fledgling community in their *History of Kentucky* (1874):

> Leestown, one mile below Frankfort, was the first spot settled by whites [in Franklin County], and as early as 1775 was a kind of stopping-place or resting-place, for the explorers or improvers from the Pitt or Mononogela country came in canoes down the Ohio and up the Kentucky River, to "look out the land." ...It is regularly laid out and flourishing.[33]

Few details are known about when the first cabins were built or whether a log stockade was erected in the area, though evidently Lee and his fellow settlers had succeeded in building a log blockhouse within the first year. When Daniel Campbell and Robert Edmiston arrived after the Indian attack of April 1776, they found a log blockhouse that had been erected to defend the settlement. Historian Willard Rouse Jillson provides a list of those identified with the formation of Leestown:

> Associated with Hancock Lee in the establishment of Leestown was [*sic*] his brother Willis Lee, Edmund Taylor, Reuben Taylor, Benjamin Ashby, John Crittenden, George Rogers Clark, Benjamin Johnson, William Eustace, John Morgan, Charles Morgan, James Blackwell.[34]

Others, including Cyrus McCracken and the large McConnell family, contributed to making the settlement a prosperous commercial center as trade along the river spread.

Despite its early prominence, Leestown was never densely populated. It was primarily a way station, a place through which people passed on their way to unclaimed land beyond the river. It also served as a convenient resting place on the road between Louisville and Lexington. After Lee's death in 1776, the town was temporarily abandoned and only lived in sporadically before the end of the war. Further setbacks to settlement came in 1777, the "Year of the Bloody Sevens," in which increased pressure by the Indians and their British allies called into question the very survival of any settlements in Kentucky. Even the weather turned enemy. The winter of 1777-1778, one of the harshest on record, froze the Kentucky River and depleted wild game severely, prompting those who were able to seek refuge in the East.

The war in the East at first slowed the rate of settlement almost to a standstill. Many, including Hancock Lee, who served in the 13th Virginia Regiment, made their way back to their original homes to lend their support to the cause of independence. Edmund and Reuben Taylor, the brothers who had accompanied Cresswell, both returned to Virginia and enlisted with their numerous brothers, both eventually serving as captains on the Continental Line. After the war, both returned to Kentucky with claims for substantial parcels of land. General George Rogers Clark prosecuted Virginia's war in the west, capturing British garrisons at Vincennes and Kaskaskia as well as attacking the Shawnee town of Piqua in what is now Ohio. No longer being identified with Leestown, he later laid out the town of Clarksville, Indiana. The small post that he established at the Falls of the Ohio in 1778 became the city of Louisville.

In the spring of 1780, a party of Indians attacked a group of salt-makers from Bryan's Station who were camped upstream at a crossing just above Benson Creek at Devil's Hollow. The only fatality was Stephen Frank, from whom, it is said, Frankfort derived its name, initially being referred to as "Franksford." [35]

Competing with Lee and others in their efforts to promote Leestown was General James Wilkinson (1757-1825), who laid out the nearby town of Frankfort, which was incorporated by the Virginia legislature in 1791. Until then, the site of Frankfort, as Wilkinson testified that year, was known as "Leestown bottom." [36] Spurred by political ambition and the hope of personal gain, Wilkinson moved rapidly to establish Frankfort as a center of trade. In 1787 he secured a charter from Virginia to operate a ferry and soon built a warehouse to accommodate goods. Though a Michael Warnick built a storehouse at Leestown (costing six pounds, four pence) as early as 1783, the establishment of a ferry crossing at the site of the future capital did much to lure travelers away from Leestown. Despite political intrigues in the so-called Spanish Conspiracy that eventually called his loyalty into question, Wilkinson for the first time successfully opened markets on the lower Mississippi by reaching a trade agreement with Don Esteban Rodriquez Miro, the Spanish governor of New Orleans. Tellingly, in naming most of the first streets in Frankfort after fellow generals as well as one for his wife Ann, Wilkinson named a street in Miro's honor, though the spelling over the years changed to Mero.

In 1787 General James Wilkinson boldly accompanied the first load of Kentucky products, on two flatboats, downriver to New Orleans. The cargo consisted of tobacco, salted hams, and butter. Halted at Natchez, Wilkinson persuaded the Spanish authorities to let the flatboats proceed, and at New Orleans he secured a treaty permitting future trade as well as a handsome profit. Soon, tobacco, smoked ham, hemp, and Kentucky bourbon were being shipped from landings and wharves along the Kentucky, including Frankfort and Leestown. The Englishman Alexander Fitzroy, describing economic opportunity in *The Country of Kentuckie in North America* (1786), noted the establishment at Lexington, Greenville, and Leestown of "inspection houses" for tobacco, "which is cultivated to great advantage, although not altogether the staple of the country."[37] In an article written in 1898 by someone described only as "a resident of Frankfort," it is said that Leestown had the first "tobacco manufactory" in Franklin County, "conducted by a gentleman named Maruce," who was known for producing a fine brand of cavendish and who was said to have done a lucrative business.[38]

Wilkinson's risk-taking paid off, for within four years of the initial trip in 1787 he sent goods valued at $100,000. This economic activity benefited Leestown as well as Frankfort. In both places warehouses were built as temporary storage for goods to be shipped, and soon whiskey joined the inventories of Kentucky products that were being transported downriver. The flatboats themselves, which were designed to be carried downstream only by the current, were broken down and salvaged for their lumber when they reached their destinations.

During this period of brisk commercial activity on the river, the first whiskey was distilled at the Leestown settlement, the beginning of a trade in spirits that fueled an economic boom for the entire region. Despite progress at the Lee settlement, the ferry that Wilkinson developed in Frankfort at what is now the foot of Wilkinson Boulevard diverted traffic from Leestown. However, as late as 1791 — the year before Kentucky was admitted to the Union — it was unclear whether Leestown would become a suburb of Frankfort or Frankfort a suburb of Leestown.

Leestown early felt the effects of its nearby rival, Frankfort, which outmaneuvered it and a half-dozen other contenders, including Lexington and Louisville, to become the state's capital in 1792. Significantly, with a few exceptions such as Louisville and Lexington, most of the proposed sites were situated along the Kentucky River — at Petersburg (close to Versailles), Ledgerwood's Bend, Delany's Ferry, Boonesborough, and Leestown. This fact underscores the perceived importance of the river as an avenue of commerce from the time of earliest settlement. Andrew Holmes' offer of land and materials to locate the capital at Frankfort eventually won out over other competitors. Frankfort's advantages of ferries, bridges, and later the railroad gradually put Leestown out of the running.

After the war and before being developed as an ideal site for a distillery, Leestown settled into a period of relative calm. As early as 1789, Hancock Lee advertised lots for sale on his claim at Leestown, but few were actually sold. Though at one time Leestown had a larger population than Frankfort, an expanding residential community did not materialize. Instead, it became the seat of the Lees, the Taylors, and their Virginia relations, who eventually looked to its commercial potential, especially its proximity to transportation routes on land and water. The abundance of pure spring water, as was soon discovered, made it an ideal site for the distillation of whiskey.

The first substantial building at Leestown of which there is a record is a stone house built by Commodore Richard Taylor (1749-1825). Though somewhat altered in appearance, it still stands on the grounds of Buffalo Trace Distillery to the west of the distillery clubhouse. While the date of its construction is uncertain — ranging from 1785 to 1792 — it is perhaps the oldest surviving structure in Franklin County. Nestled among the distillery buildings, "Riverside" is a simple stone structure to which a frame second story was later added. The builder, Commodore Richard Taylor of Orange County, Virginia, was a cousin of Hancock Taylor and Hancock Lee and the brother of Reuben and Edmund Taylor, Cresswell's colonial companions at Leestown. Nominated by the Kentucky Historical Society, the building is listed on the National Register of Historic Places. The distillery has plans to restore the house to its original appearance when it functioned as Taylor's residence and office.

Richard Taylor served his native Virginia during the Revolution as a sea captain, first commanding the armed galley *Tartar* on which he was wounded, and then the schooner *Patriot,* engaging in battle with an English vessel, the *Lord Howe,* off the Virginia coast and causing it to withdraw. In another engagement near the mouth of Chesapeake Bay, he was wounded severely in the knee, a wound from which he suffered for the rest of his life and which eventually caused his death. The injury resulted when he attacked a British ship in open boats after his own ship became becalmed. Though seriously wounded, he forced the surrender of the British crew and conducted them into Norfolk harbor. During the war he captured several British cruisers, one of which, The *Speedwell,* was sent to the West Indies for badly needed supplies and ammunition for the army. In 1787 he was given the title of Chief Officer of the Virginia Navy and awarded the honorific title of Commodore by which he was thereafter generally known. Respected and well-regarded, he was an original member of the Order of Cincinnatus, an honorary society consisting of officers of the Revolution.[39]

Though Taylor later moved to West Port in Jefferson County where he lived on 5,333 acres for his services in the Navy, he first immigrated to Leestown where Kentucky's first governor, Isaac Shelby, had appointed him Superintendent of Navigation on the Kentucky River. Assigned to promote the use of the river as an avenue of commerce, he had authority, though virtually no funds, to have the channel cleared as a means of encouraging trade. Though the channel was surveyed in 1799 and a company chartered in 1801 to clear it of debris, little was accomplished until 1818, when the state legislature finally made an appropriation to underwrite the effort.[40] One of a succession of Taylors associated with Leestown, he was the great-grandfather of E. H. Taylor, Jr., one of the vital forces in Leestown's and Kentucky's destiny as a center of the distilling industry.

Commodore Richard Taylor had two sons who also lived at Leestown for a time —"Hopping Dick" and "Black Dick," half-brothers. The second son, Richard "Black Dick" Taylor (1777-1835) — so-called for his very dark complexion — built a large brick house called "Stony Point" on Rock Hill, a site overlooking the river near or at the site where a large stone residence now dominates the distillery grounds. Having immigrated to Jefferson County, Kentucky, from Orange County, Virginia, in 1796, he moved to Frankfort in 1811, living for a time at Leestown. Grandfather of E. H. Taylor, Jr., he later moved to western Kentucky where he surveyed military land grants, dying of cholera in Columbus, Kentucky, in 1835.

The first son was "Hopping Dick" (1770-1830), a name he acquired from lameness resulting from a wound inflicted by Indians. Accounts vary. One says he was wounded on an expedition to the Indian towns with George Rogers Clark. Another states that he was wounded in battle during the Revolution. The Draper papers provide the fullest and perhaps the most plausible version. Taylor was visiting cousins in nearby Woodford County when the son of General Charles Scott was shot by Indians at Scott's Landing on the Kentucky River. Placing the body by the bank of the river as a decoy, the Indians shot Taylor in the hip when he went to rescue it. Because of the resulting limp and the need to distinguish him from his half-brother, people thereafter referred to him as "Hopping Dick."

By all accounts he was active in the civic affairs of Frankfort. In 1799 he was selected as contractor to build Kentucky's first penitentiary, a two-story stone block building with iron-barred windows and doors, located at Holmes and High Streets in North Frankfort. In 1811 he built a public warehouse for hemp, flour, and tobacco (and probably whiskey) in Leestown at the mouth of Leestown Branch. In 1814 he was appointed to a commission to find a site to build a new capitol, the first having burned the previous year. For a time he performed duties as Sergeant-at-Arms of the Court of Appeals. During the War of 1812 he served as a colonel under General James Wilkinson (after whom he named a son). While soldiering as captain of a regiment under General William Henry Harrison, the general is reported to have said, "If I wanted a man to storm the gates of hell, I would choose Dick Taylor." [41]

As proprietor of the Old Mansion House at the corner of Montgomery (now Main) and St. Clair Streets, he was charged with arranging the dinner at the hotel honoring General LaFayette during his visit to

Frankfort in 1825. By virtue of his family relations, he must have been one of the rising generation of men associated with developing Leestown. Settling in Leestown, "Hopping Dick" built a home named "Belle Font" near the distillery and the nearby spring from which his house took its name. Unfortunately, neither "Stony Point" nor "Belle Font" survived into the twentieth century. Taylors were so intimately associated with the area that some early residents referred to the settlement as Taylortown. The Taylor name continued to be identified with Leestown and the distilling industry, most notably during the nineteenth century through Black Dick's grandson, E. H. Taylor, Jr.

II.

Antebellum Leestown

Among the three earliest surviving landmarks at Leestown is "Glen Willis," the home built by Willis Atwell Lee, Jr., nephew of Hancock Lee, on an acre of land deeded him by his uncle at the time he was surveying his property in Leestown's bid to become capital of the state. In Hancock's will was a provision conveying a parcel of land at Leestown: "For the love and affection I bear my nephew, Willis Atwell Lee, and in consideration of one shilling, I give him this land, on which to build him a home." [1]

When Willis Lee was killed by Indians in 1776, Hancock Lee undertook to raise and educate his nephew, Willis Atwell Lee, Jr. (c. 1775-1824). Before he was twenty, Lee left his home in Culpepper County, Virginia, to join his uncle in Kentucky, where he took a position in the office of Judge Thomas Todd. "Glen Willis," named by Willis Lee, Jr., began in 1793 as a double two-story log house, which Lee later replaced with the imposing (though greatly modified) story-and-a-half brick home seen today on Leestown Pike (now Wilkinson Boulevard) just west of the distillery property. Designed as a "river house," its main elevation at one time faced the Kentucky and suggests how vital the river was to the community's early existence.

Having added a hundred or so acres to the property, Willis Lee died

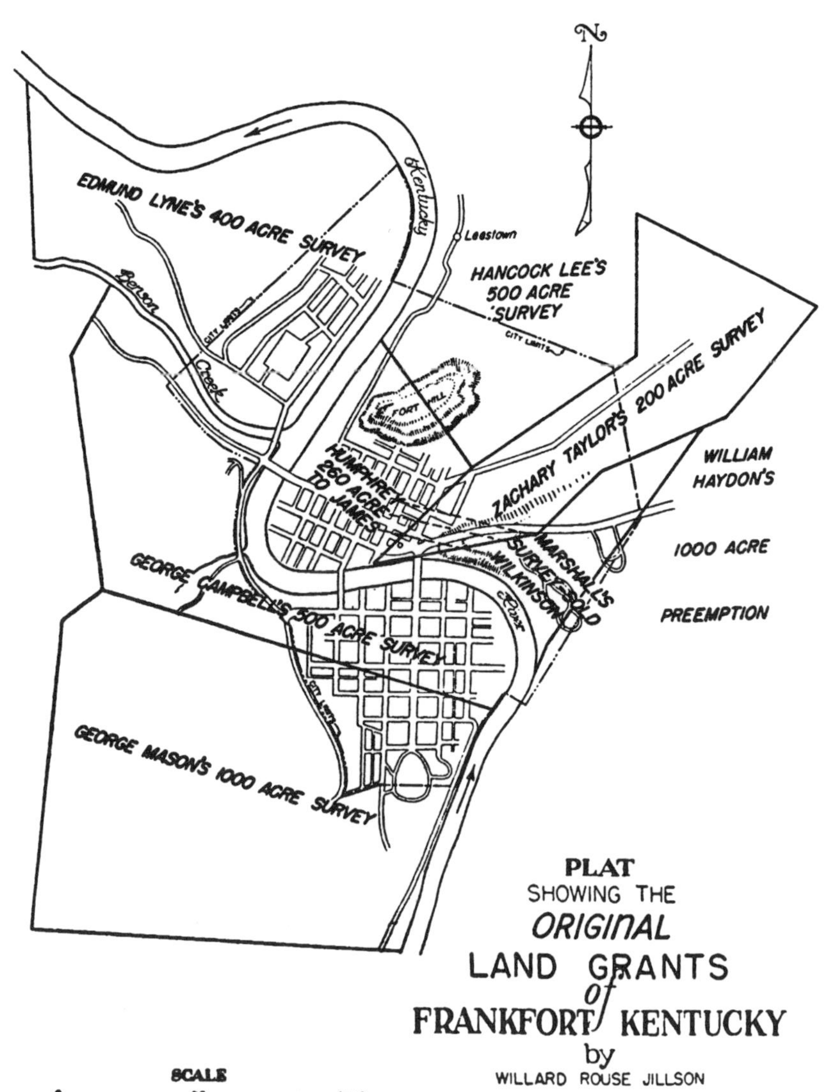

N
Kentucky
Leestown
EDMUND LYNE'S 400 ACRE SURVEY
HANCOCK LEE'S 500 ACRE SURVEY
CITY LIMITS
Benson Creek
CITY LIMITS
FORT HILL
ZACHARY TAYLOR'S 200 ACRE SURVEY
HUMPHREY'S 280 ACRE TO JAMES'S
WILLIAM HAYDON'S
1000 ACRE
PREEMPTION
MARSHALL'S SURVEY SOLD
WILKINSON
GEORGE CAMPBELL'S 500 ACRE SURVEY
GEORGE MASON'S 1000 ACRE SURVEY
PLAT
SHOWING THE
ORIGINAL
LAND GRANTS
of
FRANKFORT KENTUCKY
by
WILLARD ROUSE JILLSON
SCALE
MILE

in 1824 at age forty-nine. In 1832 his family sold the property to Humphrey Marshall (1760-1841), a revolutionary soldier, Kentucky legislator, U.S. senator, and author of *The History of Kentucky* (1812), the most popular early history of the state. Marshall lived with his family at Glen Willis until his death in 1841. A colorful, controversial lawyer and staunch Federalist, Marshall opposed the alleged attempts of General James Wilkinson to draw Kentucky away from the Union and align her with Spain. A fierce partisan, he fought a duel in 1809 with his greatest political rival Henry Clay. He squabbled and litigated unceasingly with another political foe, Judge Harry Innes. After Marshall's death and burial at a now unmarked site on his farm at Glen Willis, the property was purchased by Henry Harrison Murray (the family after whom Frankfort's Murray Street is named), a prominent local merchant and contractor. In 1887 Murray added the second story and a ballroom on the third floor. A two-story wing (since removed) was added as well, and the main entrance was reoriented toward what is now Wilkinson Boulevard.

Before Hancock Lee departed to settle land he owned at Midway (willed to him by his cousin Hancock Taylor), he sold off what remained of his original five hundred acres and deeded a ten-acre piece to Willis Atwell Lee and Richard "Hopping Dick" Taylor. Joined by John Pope, Lee and Taylor formed a partnership to lay out town lots and form a city. Among other improvements, the parties planted trees and staked off streets, hoping to draw newcomers to Leestown. Despite their efforts, the proposed town on the site did not flourish.

Hancock Lee's nephew Willis Atwell Lee was a popular and respected local personality. He served as Clerk of the Kentucky State Courts and of what was then known as the General Court. At the time of his death he served as Clerk of the Kentucky Senate, a post that put him in contact with most of the state's political leaders of the day. His political influence was such that he was selected as a Presidential Elector for Kentucky in 1817 and again in 1821. A gregarious man celebrated for his hospitality and music-making, Lee, it was said, was able "to bring more out of a fiddle than any man living." [2]

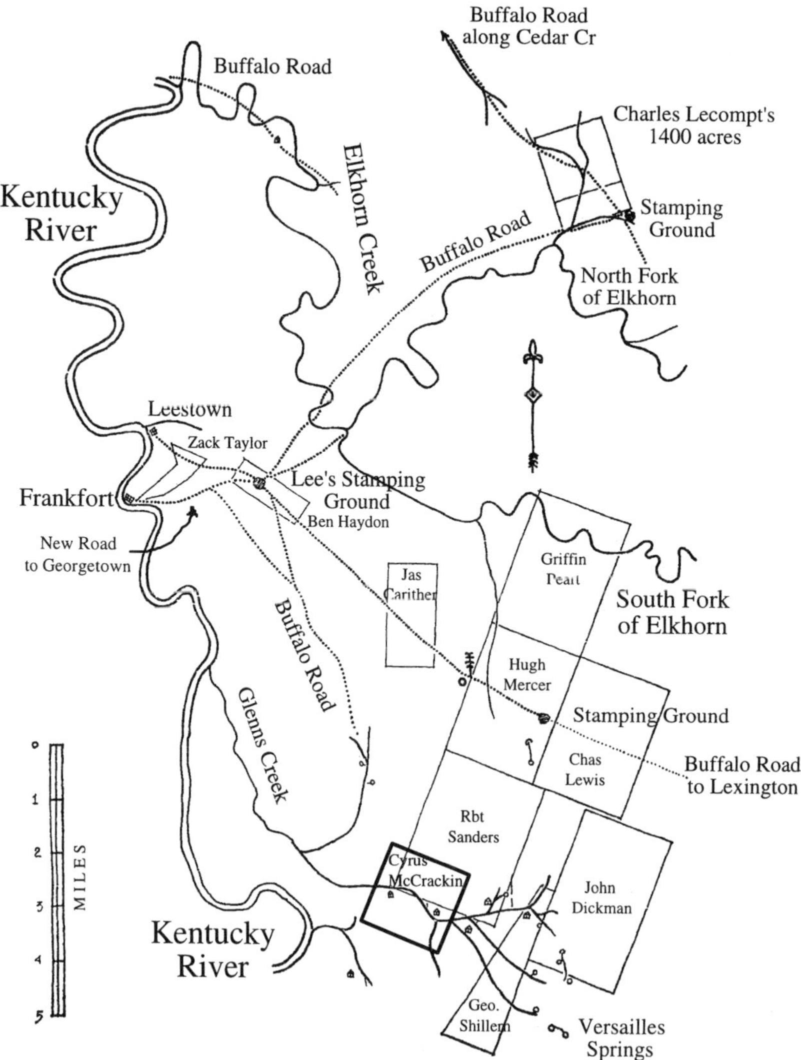

Facsimile of Survey
from Court Records
John H. Craig vs the McCracken Heirs

(Map courtesy of Neal O. Hammon)

Another landmark of early Leestown is "Beechwood," or "The Beeches," the home of the Blanton family, still lived in by the original owner's descendants. In 1818 Harrison Blanton (1791-1879), one of the earliest settlers of Leestown and later an owner of a successful building supply business, erected the fine Federal house located across from the distillery on Leestown Pike. One wing is believed to have been built as early as 1795 and was incorporated in the later structure. It contained a large basement room with a stone fireplace and was at first used as a kitchen. Reputed to have been built by masons and craftsmen in his employ, the house was constructed of bricks fired on the property. The woods used on the interior — ash floors and cherry woodwork — were selected from timber in the neighboring woods. As contractor for the Old State House, he had quarried stone "from the bed of the Kentucky River" at Leestown. The stone used for the foundation of his residence was probably taken from the same limestone ledges at the Leestown crossing.

Today's Thorn Hill, which rises three hundred feet and separates Leestown from north Frankfort, was known as "Blanton's Hill" because it was part of the family's extensive land holdings in the area. The house derived its name from the ancient American beeches that originally surrounded the house and were later replaced by European beeches and sycamores when the originals succumbed to blight. There is a family tradition that Harrison Blanton, like many of his contemporaries, distilled his own whiskey on the property.[3] Contractor, mason, quarrier, planter, he also had a strong interest in horticulture, planting apricot trees and other exotics on his property. In the side yard are the remains of an English elm he planted, a landmark reputed to have been the largest tree in Franklin County. He was also a benefactor, deeding Fort Hill to the city in 1866 on condition that it be retained as a park. Both "The Beeches" and "Glen Willis" are listed on the National Register of Historic Places.

As will be seen, the Blanton family also has strong associations with the local distilling industry. Benjamin Harrison Blanton (b. 1829), the son of Harrison Blanton, was born in Franklin County but moved to the West as a young man, settling in Denver. When the Civil War broke out, he returned to Kentucky and enlisted in the Confederate army, serving as an aide-de-camp to General John Bell Hood in Longstreet's corps of the Army of Northern Virginia. Rising from the rank of first lieutenant to major, he was described by Hood as having performed "gallant and efficient service," fighting at Second Manassas, Antietam Creek, Gettysburg, Chickamauga, Dalton, the Siege of Atlanta, Franklin, and Nashville. When the war ended, he returned to Leestown and took up residence at his boyhood home and later became closely associated with the Stagg distillery.

James Bacon Blanton (1869-1951), Benjamin's son, represented the third generation of Blantons to live at "The Beeches." He started a sand-pumping and building supply business in the early 1900s at the foot of the Second Street Bridge. Today, his daughters Alice Bacon Blanton and Anna Blanton Howell own the house, the former making it her residence.

The Blantons have maintained a long and continuous relationship with Leestown as well as its distilleries for the better part of two hundred years. James Blanton's brother, "Colonel" Albert Bacon Blanton, was associated with the Stagg distillery as one of its principal officers, accountant, and part owner during the early decades of the twentieth century, becoming a key figure in the distillery's history following E. H. Taylor, Jr. Blanton's statue stands in the park-like area outside the log clubhouse, which he had built on the distillery grounds. The mansion he built for his wife on the hill overlooking the distillery grounds now houses the executive offices for Buffalo Trace Distillery.

In addition to the Blantons, the families that formed the first industries at Leestown were Lees and Taylors. Though the sources are vague, it is probable that whiskey was distilled on the Leestown site as early as 1787. By 1814 one of the Taylors operated a sawmill at the mouth of Leestown branch. Drawing on the surrounding woodlands, it must have supplied much of the lumber used to construct buildings in the area. Though the Virginia legislature had authorized building a warehouse for the inspection of tobacco as early as 1783, it was not until 1811 that Richard Taylor built the needed warehouse. A large, three-story, stone structure erected in partnership with Willis Atwell Lee, the business was variously known as the

Leestown Warehouse, the Taylor and Lee Warehouse, or Taylor's and Lee's Warehouse. Standing on a bluff above the river for sixty years, it was finally torn down by the early George Stagg distillery and replaced with a larger structure.

During the War of 1812 Leestown served as a depot for supplies brought from the interior of the state and later shipped by flatboat to points on the Indiana shore closest to the northward march of troops under Isaac Shelby. According to one account, the "ladies of Franklin County" sent two wagon-loads of clothing for the troops. Local tradition states that the Johnson Brothers of Leestown was the headquarters for supplies being shipped to the northwestern armies.[4]

What was Leestown like during this early period? The most detailed reminiscence comes to us through Mary Willis Woodson (1819-1897), Willis Atwell Lee's granddaughter, who was born at "Glen Willis" and lived there during her early years. Her *Recollections of Frankfort* provides one of the best sources for details about Leestown (and Frankfort) circa 1830. As a child she could remember sitting on the gateposts at "Glen Willis" on county court, muster, or election days watching passers-by as they headed home in the evening. She had vivid recollections of the log cabins in the Leestown area:

> In my imagination I see them, perfectly embowered in wild climbing roses, lilacs and altheas, honeysuckles, and cinnamon roses seeming to be clamering [*sic*] for possession, daffodils, jonquills, hyacinths and star of Bethlehem, scattered every where, and the great old apple trees with their ample shade. And through the branches of the sycamores, the glimmering and glistening of the river as it rippled over its smooth rocky bed.[5]

There are memories of swimming in the river, corn shuckings, the death of her Grandfather Lee, food fests, and school. She described two ways to travel from Leestown to Frankfort, one through a beautiful beech grove called "Lovers' Retreat" along the river near the "never failing" spring in the upper end of the grove. The other followed the so-called "Hill Road," which passed the roadside front of "Glen Willis," around Fort Hill, and entered Frankfort at North St. Clair Street.

One of the first steamboats to ply the Kentucky River was built at Leestown in 1811 and departed regularly after the "spring rise" for Louisville and New Orleans. Until Lock Four was built in 1840 at a cost of $120,000, Leestown was the furthermost point that steamboats could reliably travel up the Kentucky. A short distance upriver from the warehouse built by Lee and Taylor was a shallow bar known as "Lee's Ripple." It dropped off into a deep channel that became turbulent during high water and made navigation difficult and perilous. The wharf located at what was then known as Taylortown occupies the site where Buffalo Trace Distillery now stands.

As the quality of transport improved—from canoe to flatboat to keelboat to steamboat and river packet—Leestown remained a principal port for Frankfort and the surrounding area during the early decades of the nineteenth century. An enormous quantity and variety of goods came in and went out. Among the goods in warehouses at Leestown and Frankfort in 1819 were tobacco, baled rope, candles, paper, bacon, spun yarn, beef and pork, bagging soap, paper, powder, and 2,148 barrels of whiskey. Coming into Frankfort and Leestown were hogsheads of sugar, barrels of salt, iron, boxes of salmon, fish, earthenware, pecans, nails, barrels of porter, and an assortment of dry goods and groceries.[6] These hogsheads would be sterilized by fire, then used to store and ship whiskey to various destinations via steamboat along the waterways of the eastern United States.

The *Frankfort Commentator* contains one of the earliest references to a steamboat at Leestown. On Saturday, February 19, 1820, the two-hundred-ton steam *George Madison* of Louisville, commanded by Captain William T. Pemberton, tied up at Frankfort:

> The river being full, the citizens had an opportunity of witnessing for the first time, the operations of a Steam Boat before our town. She returned on the same day, as far as Leestown for the

purpose of receiving her loading, and left that place on Monday,
the 21st for New Orleans. We understand she was loaded by Col.
J. Johnson, with supplies for the government.[7]

Colonel James Johnson of Scott County, the brother of U.S. Vice-President Richard M. Johnson, was the proprietor of a freight line that operated the steamboat *Providence,* which carried freight on the Kentucky between Leestown and New Orleans when the river was navigable. At times of low water during the summer months Lee's Ripple was reduced to a trickle, and Mary Willis Woodson and her playmates often swam in the river at this spot.

As an ad in Lexington's *Kentucky Reporter* indicates, Leestown played an important role in the regular freight service to New Orleans that began as early as the summer of 1820: "On the first rise of water in the Kentucky River the steamboat *Providence* will leave Leestown one mile below Frankfort for New Orleans and will be able to carry from 150 to 200 tons of freight."[8] After 1840, when the lock and dam at Leestown went in, the volume of trade gradually diminished because the natural obstacles to navigating farther upstream were largely removed and commercial activity extended to landings farther upriver.

Ebenezer Stedman (1808-1885), owner of a paper mill on Elkhorn Creek four miles from Leestown, gives a glimpse of Leestown from the river during the 1830s when he traveled downriver from Frankfort to deliver a load of wrapping paper to Louisville. Like the distilleries at Leestown, his business, which was powered by water, suffered from fire and flood. Though his spelling is quaintly phonetic ("wrapping," for example, is "ropping"), his reminiscences are among the most insightful views into Bluegrass life during the antebellum period. Among the men he knew in Frankfort he mentions Edmund H. Taylor (Edmund, Jr.'s adoptive uncle) and Harrison Blanton of Leestown. The Leestown entry, which was written much later in life for the benefit of his daughter Nellie Cox of Franklin County, most likely dates from the mid- or late 1830s. The season was spring. Though he intended to ship his paper aboard a steamboat at Frankfort, the water was too low for the steamboat to reach that far upriver, so he was forced to transport it by keelboat twenty miles downriver to a landing in Owen County where it was loaded aboard the steamboat *Sylph*, which transported it to Louisville. Accompanying him on the keelboat, which had no accommodation for passengers, was the "Roughest Set of men I ever saw… Evry [*sic*] word was an oath." He first makes reference to the boatmen under Captain Burns poling through a narrow channel at Benson Creek past a sandbar, then has a brief description of the river at Leestown:

> Safely through This Rapid Shute we Soon Enter Another whare the Lock now stands. To me as the boat Enterd [it] look[ed] like distruction. The Chanel was on the Right hand Shore as we went down & Such Roaring of the watter, Such a swift Currant that took the Boat through like a Shot out of a Shovel. Now we are opposite the Leestown warehouse. In the Leestown pool the watter is deep, but little Curant. The Boats Moves Slow. The Captain Points out to me on the Bank whare a Number of Steam Boats have Bin Built, Some of them of Black Locus. The names i have forgotten of the Boats But Some of the ways are thare Still… Leestown was named after a man by the name of Lee. This was decided in the Cout in a suit Brot, I think, By Governor Greenup For the land whare Mary tod lives & at one time it was a Great Shipping point.

Stedman ends his Leestown references with a tantalizing afterthought: "I Could give the History of Leestown But it is not nesary [*sic*] to do So hear." 9

What Stedman instead gives is random detail and a flavor of the place — its history as a boat-building center and shipping point, the manners and character of the boatwrights and stevedores who must have been employed there. The editors of his published journal note that Stedman is referring to the tobacco-inspection warehouse that Hancock Lee built in 1783.

In 1842 the first five locks on the Kentucky were opened, creating ninety-five miles of slack water beginning at the mouth of the river at Carrollton. With the opening of the locks came year-round navigation and greater possibilities for the water transport of travelers and products. As might be expected, the importance of Leestown naturally diminished when upstream navigation was extended. After Frankfort won over Leestown and other competitors to become the state capital in the early 1790s, Leestown began to lose its vigor as a serious economic rival to Frankfort, yet it formed an ideal location for the production of bourbon whiskey, a potential that was to be fully realized during the second half of the nineteenth century.

III.

Leestown Distilling: The Early Years

No ONE KNOWS WHO produced the first bourbon whiskey in Kentucky because records were scant and distilling was widespread, almost a claim of heritage among those who settled the Ohio River Valley. The name put forward most often is that of the Reverend Elijah Craig (1743-1808), the celebrated Baptist preacher and early entrepreneur of Scott County who once used Kentucky as a metaphor for heaven: "Oh, my honeys, heaven is a Kentucky of a place." Legend suggests that he invented the process of making bourbon whiskey by accident, discovering that aging the liquid in charred kegs imparted its distinctive taste and reddish color. Another legend alleges that a jug of his product was ensconced in one of the brick columns of Giddings Hall at Georgetown College.

From the earliest years of settlement, one established fact spurred the production of Kentucky Bourbon among the region's farmers: corn is more valuable in its liquid form than bagged as grain. For an equally practical reason, corn won out over rye as the primary grain for whiskey production. Unlike its cousin, corn could be grown among the stumps of the cleared forests. As a small grain, rye required broad fields and larger plantings less suited to the smaller farms in the Kentucky country. Another argument in favor of converting corn to its liquid form was the economy of weight and bulk. Four bushels was the maximum load a pack horse could carry. When the grain was distilled, the same horse could carry the equivalent of twenty-four bushels, or forty gallons of whiskey.

Who made the first whiskey in Kentucky is a question that probably will never be resolved because distilling was such a widespread practice. For example, pioneer William Calk, among the first settlers at Boonesborough in 1775, brought his distilling equipment with him from Virginia, as did countless others. Other candidates for distilling the first bourbon whiskey in Kentucky are Jacob Meyers and Jacob Froman (Lincoln County), Jacob Spears (Bourbon County), and Marsham Brashear (Jefferson County). By 1780 James Pepper, one of the early leaders in the industry, had established his distillery at Lexington. In the Outer Bluegrass near Bardstown, Jacob Beam, patriarch of the Beam distilling family, set up a still in 1788. The Samuels family, known now for the production of Maker's Mark at Loretto, Kentucky, began making whiskey in the 1780s. Isaac Shelby, Kentucky's first governor, owned a going distillery when he entered office in 1792. One source claims that Elijah Pepper is reported to have set up a still near Frankfort as early as 1778.[1] As for who among the early claimants made it first, it is just as likely that some unnamed individual operating in obscurity deserves the distinction, for whiskey was relatively easy to make. The challenge was making good whiskey. Bourbon whiskey, as it was then produced, required only minimal apparatus and some knowledge of fundamentals.

In the beginning, the process of whiskey-making was so rudimentary that the farmer-distiller could install his entire operation in a one-room building, often a crude shack. First, the grain was ground to a coarse flour, either by an animal treadmill or a water wheel. The mixture of water and grain was stirred by hand in wooden tubs similar to the common hogshead. These tubs often doubled as fermenting vats. Generally, copper stills were used, and often a second still was used to redistill the first still's output, a procedure that improved the quality. The late Laurence Thompson, director of the UK library and scholar of early Kentucky, summarized the basic formula for distilling Kentucky bourbon:

Corn for strength and body, rye for mellow flavor, aging in charred oak barrels for amber color. Bourbon is made from a fermented mash containing at least 51% corn and lesser amounts of wheat [or] rye, and barley, along with yeast and distilled limestone water. It is distilled at no more than 160 proof and aged in [new] charred oak barrels, giving the bourbon its reddish color and unique taste.[2]

By 1811 nearly two thousand registered distilleries were operating in Kentucky, and who knows how many unregistered ones. They produced 2.2 million wine gallons a year. Because whiskey was so common from the time of earliest settlement, the origins of whiskey-making in Kentucky are shrouded in myth. Records of the industry are sparse and incomplete. The name "bourbon" very likely derives from Bourbon County (covering a large portion of central Kentucky and established in 1785), a name perhaps adopted from the stamping of barrels from that area of central Kentucky with the name or the number of distillers concentrated there — a process by which the product came to be identified with a specific place. At first known by such names as "western whiskey" and "Kentucky whiskey," the name by which it was most often known after the Civil War was "Bourbon whiskey."

Bourbon County, the fifth to be formed (1785), occupied an enormous area in which much of the early bourbon whiskey was distilled. Ironically, the county itself was named in honor of France's royal family at a time when the French — arguably the world's greatest makers of wine — were much admired for their support of the Revolution, a few short years before the supporters of American Revolution became themselves the victims of revolution.

Clearly, whiskey was the preferred beverage on the frontier, a fact that fueled the art of whiskey making. Far from its origins in the uplands of the British Isles, it moved west to Kentucky from Virginia, Maryland, and Pennsylvania with the first settlers. Many of those who immigrated to the Kentucky country shared an ancient tradition of whiskey making from

Ireland, Scotland, or Germany. As James E. Pepper observed, "In nearly every family liquor was a daily article of consumption, and the brown jug [was] an indispensable adjunct to labor on every occasion. No commerce was conducted in alcoholic liquors in farming regions, each man creating his own supply."

In 1791, Congress, urged on by Treasury Secretary Alexander Hamilton, placed an excise tax on whiskey, ultimately driving thousands of Scotch-Irish from Pennsylvania into the Ohio River Valley where enforcement was more difficult and resentment more keen. When Pennsylvanians refused to pay the tax, President George Washington raised an army of 13,000 — larger than any army he commanded during the Revolution — to put down the so-called Whiskey Rebellion. Levying a tax is one thing, but collecting it is another. Down the river came a constant stream of flatboats loaded with farmer/distillers and their stills. In Kentucky, where public opinion was opposed to central authority, many citizens did not cotton to tax collectors. Their papers were often stolen, their horses' ears cropped. At least once, effigies of tax collectors were hanged in Lexington.[3]

The influx of newcomers, many of them inveterate distillers, added to the impetus in the "West" to convert grain into spirits, ushering in an era of high demand. During the 1790s, the whiskey industry expanded and experimented, especially in the "corridor" between Louisville and Bardstown and between Lexington and Frankfort.[4] Though rye had been the primary grain in Pennsylvania, corn, more plentiful and easier to grow, became the primary ingredient in Kentucky. When the corn and lesser quantities of other grains were combined with pure limestone water, the result was Kentucky bourbon.

Citizens in Franklin County quickly acquired the knowledge "to turn their surplus corn into a liquid asset." [5] One indication of the health of the distilling industry in Franklin County was the litigation growing out of the federal government's attempts to impose the whiskey tax. Unsuccessful in gaining full compliance, government tax collectors finally filed a lawsuit to compel distillers to pay an excise on distilled spirits. Many distillers in Franklin and other Bluegrass counties simply refused to pay the tax.

U.S. District Judge Harry Innes, who lived near Leestown on Elkhorn Creek in Franklin County, was charged with prosecuting the suit. Of the 177 distillers named as defendants in the action, Franklin County tied with Mason County in having the fourth-greatest number of operators of "illicit stills." Those with more were Fayette, Scott, and Bourbon Counties.[6] One consequence of the so-called Whiskey Rebellion was that many Pennsylvania distillers migrated west and south to escape regulation, increasing the store of distilling know-how as well as the number of distillers in Kentucky.

Fourteen distillers from Franklin County finally paid fines for their earlier defiance of the whiskey tax. One of the holdouts was James Graham of Frankfort. Between 1860 and 1870, another James Graham, probably a descendant, worked at the distillery that occupied the site of today's Buffalo Trace distillery. The record is vague because, unfortunately, the court records were lost in the flood of 1937.

Though whiskey production increased, lack of a means to transport the finished product remained an obstacle to commerce in frontier Kentucky. Early roads were often impassable, many of them (including those at Leestown) simply adapted from game trails and buffalo traces. Limited at first to wagons and pack horses, Kentucky farmers were hard put to ship their goods to market. They were at the mercy of the weather and the practical difficulty of shipping goods east across the mountains, an undertaking both hazardous and expensive. Urban markets west of the mountains were distant, comparatively small, and relatively few.

To make matters worse, locally there were more producers than consumers, an imperfect formula for economic success. Next to water, whiskey was perhaps the most common beverage on the frontier. In a country where there were few doctors and many folk practitioners, the red elixir was regarded as a cure-all. It was an indispensable part of every "well-regulated" household, administered for whooping cough, for measles, for colds, for fevers, and for a host of other ailments, real and imagined. Most of the population were self-sufficient farmers, many of them operating their own stills. Because local markets were limited, Leestown and other locations along the river offered a ready solution for the problem of transport, especially after 1787 when James Wilkinson successfully opened southern markets as a destination for Kentucky products.

Almost from the beginning, whiskey was produced at the future site of Buffalo Trace Distillery. It has been claimed that whiskey was first made at Leestown as early as 1787. Local traditions hold that Harrison Blanton, the founder of the construction-materials business which supplied the "Kentucky Marble" used to build the "Old" State Capitol and one of the largest landowners in the Leestown neighborhood, set up a small distillery at the site of Leestown sometime in the early 1800s. If he produced a surplus beyond his family's needs, very likely he availed himself of the river as means of marketing his whiskey and the limestone water of the branch flowing from nearby Cedar Cove Spring as a means of making it.

Leestown Branch, which flowed from Cedar Cove Spring, offered a reliable source of pure water so necessary for any distilling operation. The springs also served as the source of Frankfort's drinking waterworks, having been started in 1804 by Richard Throckmorton, who laid bored cedar pipes along the Brown's bottom through Leestown into Frankfort.[7] Since Lee and Taylor's warehouse was convenient to his still, Blanton had a ready means of storing his barreled whiskey prior to shipment. River warehouses at Frankfort were only a mile or so away, so facilities at Leestown and Frankfort provided local producers with adequate and convenient places to store their goods, including whiskey, in preparation for shipment to Louisville, New Orleans, Natchez, and other markets to the south. As steamboats made it practical to ship goods up the Ohio River to Cincinnati, Pittsburgh, and destinations to the east, the market range expanded.

Once the advantages were recognized, merchants and wholesalers wasted little time in establishing whiskey as a profitable commodity. For example, merchant John James Audubon, America's greatest painter of birds, shipped three hundred barrels of whiskey for which he paid twenty-five cents per gallon from Henderson to St. Genevieve, Missouri, where it sold for two dollars per gallon.[8]

In fact, the demand was ripe for a cornucopia of produce and goods emanating from Bluegrass farmers. An 1819 warehouse inventory[9] from the Leestown warehouse suggests the variety and volume of commodities transported on the river:

EXPORTED

10,350 bbls. flour
1,374 bbls whiskey
1,985 bbls. beef & pork
10 hhds. tobacco
500 bbls. lard
427 bbls. manufactured tobacco
1,000 pieces bagging
1,568 coils rope
7 cables
20,000 lbs. bacon
18 do. soap
965 reams paper
800 kegs powder

ON HAND

1,000 bbls. flour
20 bbls. whiskey
300 bbls. beef and pork
22 hhds. tobacco
50 bbls. lard
100 bbls. manufactured tobacco
300 pieces bagging
3,000 coils rope
1 cable
80 boxes candles

Including the two other river warehouses in the area, a total of 2,148 barrels of whiskey were shipped downriver in 1818. As early as 1820, shippers advertised freight service on the Kentucky River to southern markets.

Though changeable conditions on the river — snags, deadheads, shifting currents, sandbars, rocky shoals, submerged islands — made transport hazardous and schedules subject to change, service by water increasingly became a part of the area's commercial fabric. By 1820 at least seven steamboats provided regular service on the river, and notices of departures were regularly printed.[10] The *Western Citizen* reported in February 1821 that the Kentucky "had been passable for steam-boats for nearly three weeks." The same article reported that "the steamboats Johnson and Calhoun, Captains Mcguire and Craig, have been up and taken on cargoes, the former at

Frankfort and the latter at Leestown." It was also noted that "one wheel of the Calhoun was damaged by the drift in the Ohio." In the fall of 1829 a steamboat named The *Sylph,* attempting to pass the "old ford near Frankfort," had to back down the river because the way was blocked by a heavily loaded, oxen-drawn wagon bogged down in midstream.[11]

The 1840s marked the heyday of steamboat trade on the Kentucky River. When the building of five locks was completed in 1842, slackwater navigation was possible for ninety-five miles from the river's mouth at Carrollton. Lock No. 4, located just above Leestown and Bellepoint on the west side of the river, made Frankfort accessible to steamboat navigation year-round instead of keeping it dependent on "tides" of high water during the spring and winter seasons.

Though Leestown lost its early eminence as new landings proliferated upriver, it remained a major loading point for the barrels of locally produced whiskey distilled at Leestown and other sites. During the 1850s freight and passenger transport along the river would give way to the up-and-coming railroad system, which was slowly but steadily extending into the river basin. By the 1870s, rail transport would reduce the river trade from a torrent to a trickle.

Whiskey production also evolved. By the 1820s the making of whiskey had advanced from a "domestic handicraft" to a fullblown industry, capable of producing barrel after barrel of bourbon of certified quality. Having ready access to a usually navigable river, the makers had the capability of transporting it to distant markets. Shipping more freight by water than any other source, the distilling industry dominated the river trade until the last quarter of the century, though railroads, which entered Kentucky in the 1830s, steadily ate into the volume of freight conveyed by water.

As transportation became more diversified and sophisticated, so did whiskey production. The individual farmer-distiller began to give way to an industrial system in which producers capitalized and employed skilled master distillers capable of producing greater quantities of high-quality whiskey. As early as 1807, newspapers in the Bluegrass carried ads seeking to employ experienced distillers. As in many other areas of production, the domestic system of manufacture gradually gave way to organized industry in which capitalized companies owning the means of production and employing wage-earners, many of them highly skilled, turned out a highly desirable product in greater quantities. Whiskey-making progressed from an improvised means for local farmers to dispose of their surplus corn to a value-added liquid asset in demand along all the established trade routes.

On average, an acre of distilled corn yielded about a barrel of whiskey. From simply one of many activities in which a farmer engaged, whiskey-making evolved as a specialized process with scientifically improved means of production. As early Bluegrass distiller James E. Pepper affirmed, whiskey-making had its roots among Kentucky's first generation of farmers —"a small kettle and a [still] worm placed alongside his log cabin were almost as essential a part of the farmer's household equipment as a flail for his grain or a plow for his lands." Undeniably, the area was ideal for the production of whiskey. Corn — the crop that most settlers planted on their first cleared ground — grew well. The countryside was well-watered by numerous, small, spring-fed creeks whose ample waters were relatively free of iron and ran cold enough most of the year "to condense the alcoholic vapors coursing through the still worm." [12] Even the manufactured components needed to distill alcohol were readily available. By the 1790s local coppersmiths were advertising the sale of distilling equipment. And whiskey-makers soon exploited available opportunities.

One of the early innovators in the industry was Dr. James Crow, a medical graduate of the University of Edinburgh who immigrated to Woodford County, Kentucky, in the 1820s. Having an interest in chemistry, he brought scientific measure and method to the fermentation process. He also advocated the aging of whiskey to improve its quality and was among the first to age it purposely in charred oak barrels and to practice the sour mash process of whiskey-making. His legacy was not lost upon his successors in the trade, among them Col. Edmund H. Taylor, Jr., who was to combine early lessons of production with a genius at organizing capital and salesmanship to help create the modern distilling industry.

IV.

Whiskey Comes of Age

Not until after the Civil War did the whiskey industry in Kentucky enter its first golden era as a fullblown, national industry. During the war many small distilleries were raided, and their granaries and stock were depleted by both sides. During General Braxton Bragg's invasion of Kentucky in the fall of 1862, Frankfort was under Confederate control for a short time, when Colonel John Scott's cavalry entered the city, declared it captured (the only non-Confederate capital taken by Confederate forces during the war), and hoisted the Stars and Bars above the State Capitol. Though troops were under strict orders not to disturb private property, Bragg's forces insisted on purchasing goods with Confederate currency that was practically worthless. Among the commercial entities that suffered was the Frankfort Woolen Factory from which the Confederates appropriated 74,960 yards of Kentucky Jeans and for which the company received deflated Confederate currency.[1] The Leestown distillery was not raided, but thirsty Confederate troops passed dangerously close during their retreat from Frankfort to rejoin the retreating Confederate army at the end of Bragg's campaign, the last serious Southern attempt to take Kentucky.

To protect the city, Federal authorities located a fortified earthworks and command post on nearby Blanton's Hill (thereafter known as Fort Hill) from which local militia and Union troops repulsed another take-over of the capital city during June 1864. This time a detachment from General John Hunt Morgan's cavalry approached Fort Hill close by the distillery, one party advancing up the rear of Fort Hill along the Owenton road, a short distance from the distillery. The defenses atop the hill were assaulted on June 10, but after two days of probing attacks and determined Union resistance the Confederate forces were forced to withdraw. They failed to secure the arms and munitions that were housed in the State Arsenal and to dislodge the federal defenders at Fort Boone atop the hill overlooking the distillery grounds on one side and the city of Frankfort on the other.[2]

The end of the war signaled an expansive period of growth and progress for Kentucky distillers, and one of the best examples of this modernizing trend occurred at Leestown. The legacy of the early bourbon makers was passed on to a new generation of distillers and entrepreneurs, who consolidated the lessons learned about the art of whiskey-making and established the means to market Kentucky bourbon to the nation and the world.

One of the new developments in this process was the rise of distributors who marketed the final product for resale at its final destination. Through one such firm Edmund Haynes Taylor, Jr. (1830-1923) — one of the geniuses of the industry — got his start. A descendant of the early Taylors who had figured importantly in the settlement of Leestown, Taylor's great-uncle was General Zachary Taylor, hero of the Mexican War and later president (1849-50). His great-grandfather was Commodore Richard Taylor, whose stone house, as previously mentioned, survived over two centuries of change and growth at the distillery site. His grandfather, Richard "Black Dick" Taylor, Jr., was Government Surveyor of the Jackson Purchase in western Kentucky.

Born in Columbus, Kentucky, on February 12, 1830 (Lincoln's birthday) to John E. Taylor and Rebecca Edrington Taylor, Edmund H. Taylor was orphaned at an early age, going first to live with his great-uncle Zachary in Baton Rouge, Louisiana, where the future president commanded the

Southwest Department of the U.S. Army. Well-educated for the day, young Edmund was sent to Boyer's French School in New Orleans before coming to Frankfort, where he was adopted and raised by his uncle E. H. Taylor, Sr. One of Frankfort's most prominent community leaders, Col. Edmund H. Taylor (1799-1873) had served on the committee in Frankfort to raise money by lottery for the municipal water system (from Cove Spring) as well as a public school. In addition to being a successful banker, he operated a ferry at Frankfort. To keep from being confused with his prominent uncle, the younger Edmund Taylor added the "Jr." to his name. In Frankfort he completed a classical education at B. B. Sayre's Academy (which later moved to Lexington). Seeing opportunities in banking, he entered the Branch Bank of Kentucky at Frankfort headed by his uncle Edmund H. Taylor. At twenty he opened branch banks at Paducah and Harrodsburg, later becoming head of the branch in Versailles. Building on his successes, he later opened the private bank of Taylor, Turner & Co. in Lexington. At age twenty-one, he married Fannie Johnson, daughter of William Stapleton Johnson of Frankfort.

Though E. H. Taylor, Jr., had a knack for handling money, banking was only a prelude to his entry into the distilling industry. Having personally known many of the early whiskey-makers, he was soon drawn to distilling and informed himself about all aspects of the industry. In the early 1860s he gave up banking and helped form the firm of Gaines, Berry & Company, distillers. Though he never donned a uniform, Taylor served the Union cause during the Civil War as a purchasing agent. Several members of the Taylor family joined the Confederacy (including his playmate General Richard Taylor, the president's son). Though his exact role isn't clear, he probably procured whiskey for the U.S. Army since spirits at the time were a part of every soldier's daily rations.

In 1868, shortly after the death of Oscar Pepper, he organized the firm of W. A. Gaines & Co., which connected itself with James Pepper, the late Oscar Pepper's son. The firm became successors to the Crow and Pepper names as respected brands. Taylor, along with his partners William Gaines and Hiram Berry, leased the old Pepper distillery and began to make whiskey in response to the greater demand following the Civil War as the country expanded and the movement westward regained its momentum.

Taylor's association with distilling at Leestown began in 1869 when he built the O.F.C. (Old Fire Copper) and Carlisle distilleries situated at the current site of Buffalo Trace Distillery. Ten years later, he and the Gaines Company constructed a new distillery for Old Crow, rebuilding and modernizing the Pepper on Glenn's Creek. Known as the Old Taylor Distillery, it resembled a castle built in a creek bottom, a Gothic brick complex in the form of a feudal fortress. Outside, it was carefully landscaped with gardens and pools that gave it an air of never-never land. Inside, it contained the most up-to-date distilling equipment, capable of producing a sanitary product in a practically antiseptic environment.[3]

Though less impressive aesthetically than the Old Taylor complex, the two Leestown distilleries, located about a quarter-mile below Lock and Dam No. 4, were state-of-the-art facilities, their fermenting rooms built of white-washed limestone containing the best distilling equipment "that money could buy." The O.F.C. distillery advertised that it was "the only distillery where the product is in contact with copper alone from the time the grain is ground until the finished whiskey is barreled in the splendid oak packages made at the company's cooper shops from selected and seasoned timber." This dedication to copper became a Taylor trademark.

The third distillery that Taylor built during these years was Hermitage Distillery in South Frankfort, an area that was only sparsely developed at the time. Located on the Kentucky River between Second and Cross Streets, the now-defunct distillery is visible on the 1871 bird's-eye view map of Frankfort. In addition to the distilling buildings, it consisted of seven warehouses and a cooperage. Situated on a river plain like its sisters at Leestown, it was also susceptible to flooding.

L.F. Johnson in *The History of Franklin County* (1912) praises Taylor's contributions to the distilling industry and offers a general assessment of his contributions to the industry:

It was not until after the close of the Civil War, about the year

An early artist depicted legendary explorer and pioneer Daniel Boone (1734-1820) overlooking a herd of migrating buffalo. Thousands of buffalo once moved throughout Kentucky, migrating from fresh water springs to salt licks in various regions. Their migration established a network of trails or "traces" that eventually led pioneers and settlers to new adventures and new homes.

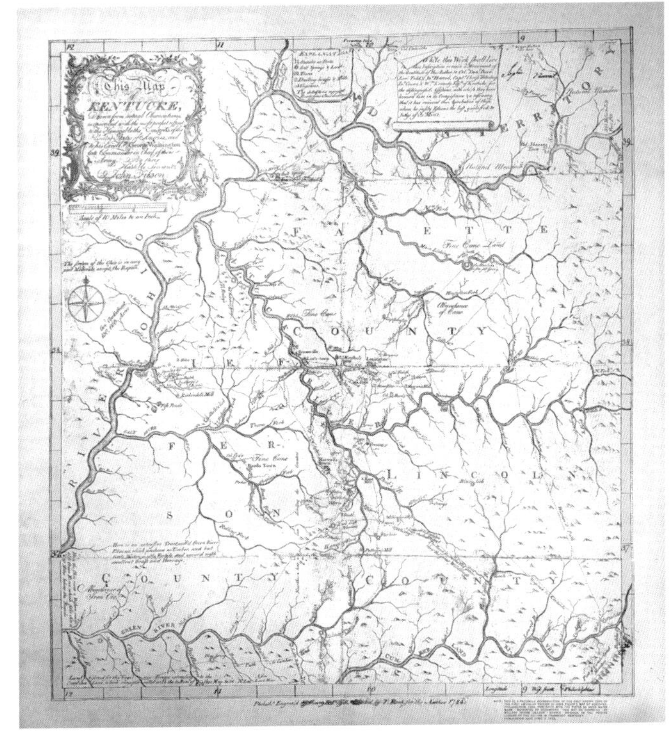

In 1784, explorer and surveyor John Filson (1753-1788) provided the first map document of Kentucky, which at the time was still part of Virginia. Not only did it depict Kentucky's natural waterways and existing counties, but it also indicated the network of buffalo traces, including the Great Buffalo Trace that led northward to the Kentucky River. Eleven years before Filson's map, pioneers followed this trace to the ancient buffalo crossing at the river where they established Lee's Town, the first settlement north of the Kentucky River in 1773. Today, this same site is home to Buffalo Trace Distillery.

This early lithograph depicts the first modern distillery that was built on the Lee's Town site (today's home of the Buffalo Trace Distillery) in 1857. It was the first U.S. distillery to incorporate the use of steam power, which was a major advance in producing high quality whiskey. The lithograph incorporates the distillery's original source of limestone spring water, fed by the Cove Spring Branch.

E.H. Taylor, Jr. purchased the distillery at Lee's Town in 1870 and named his new operation "O.F.C." derived from "old fire copper," which was an early name for the type of still used by Taylor. Soon its reputation for producing fine whiskey spread throughout the United States and parts of Europe. The O.F.C. name was so synonymous with quality whiskey that several other producers tried to pass their wares off under the same name.

E.H. Taylor, Jr. is pictured here in this early lithograph of the O.F.C. steam room. Under Taylor's direction, O.F.C. pioneered the use of steam in whiskey production. Taylor was an industry leader who greatly advanced the quality of Kentucky's bourbon and safeguarded the bourbon label from bogus producers.

A second distillery, "Carlisle," was built adjacent to the O.F.C. operation between 1879-1880. Comprised of the two distilleries, the property was among the largest and the finest in the world. By 1890, six warehouses held storage space for more than 70,000 barrels.

Lightning struck and burned the O.F.C. distillery in 1882. Reconstruction of the flagship plant began immediately and the new distillery was larger and greatly improved at a cost of rebuilding at $44,762.58 over and above insurance collected – a considerable sum for that day and time.

Different trade mark brands produced by the distillery in barrels ready for shipment.

The first known photograph of the distillery, taken in 1896, shows Warehouses A, B, and C, which still stand today, as well as Lewis Ferry Road, which runs through the distillery grounds.

Colonel E. H. Taylor, Jr. at his distillery office in the 1880s.

This photo, taken in 1897, shows the distillery's on-site cooperage, which helped ensure higher quality control for the barrels in which O.F.C. whiskey would be aged.

This early photograph depicts the main entrance to the distillery on Lewis Ferry Road (circa 1905). Distillery workers are pictured here with barrels of O.F.C. whiskey.

Albert B. Blanton, who
grew up on a farm
adjacent to the O.F.C.
distillery, came to work
at the facility in 1897.
He eventually became
the Master Distiller and
retired in 1952.

Albert B. Blanton, a bourbon aristocrat in the mold of
E. H. Taylor, Jr. and the great whiskey men of the 1800s,
took pride in the distillery as well as its products. In 1933-34
he designed and built the stately Stony Point Mansion
pictured here, which overlooks the distillery grounds.

Rising waters of the Kentucky River engulfed the distillery during the Great Flood of 1937. The river rose 17 feet above the first floor elevation of the distillery's riverside power plant and four feet above the first floor of the Warehouse H, well back from the riverbank. As the waters began to recede, Col. Blanton restored normal operations within 24 hours.

By 1943, technology, economics, and environmental concerns brought about the construction of a "dry house" on the distillery grounds where the spent grain was dried and sold as a protein-rich ingredient for all types of animal feed. Albert Blanton is shown here helping lay the foundation.

Warehouse C at Buffalo Trace Distillery was built in 1885, and reportedly ages the distillery's best whiskeys.

Elmer T. Lee, special consultant and Master Distiller Emeritus for Buffalo Trace Distillery, has served the distillery for more than 50 years.

In 1953 the distillery marked the production of its 2 millionth barrel since the 1933 repeal of Prohibition by building the world's only one-barrel bonded warehouse.

The distillery site has withstood 9 major floods over the last two centuries, including the one shown here in this 1957 photograph.

The distillery flourished and grew throughout the 1950s and 1960s. By 1961 the distillery incorporated 3 miles of railroad and 16 warehouses.

This buffalo sculpture, carved in 1999 by Kentucky artist Stan Schu from a fallen 300-year-old sycamore tree, commemorates the distillery's buffalo heritage.

A hand-laid stone entrance greets visitors at Buffalo Trace Distillery, which was officially renamed in 1999 in honor of the Great Buffalo Trace crossing that was once located on the distillery grounds by the Kentucky River.

The Buffalo Trace Distillery Clubhouse was named in honor of Master Distiller Emeritus Elmer T. Lee. The Clubhouse and Gardens were designed by Albert B. Blanton and are open to visitors year-round.

A statue honoring the memory and legacy of Albert B. Blanton graces the great lawn by the distillery's Clubhouse.

Buffalo Trace Kentucky Straight Bourbon Whiskey, introduced in 1999, is the distillery's namesake and flagship product.

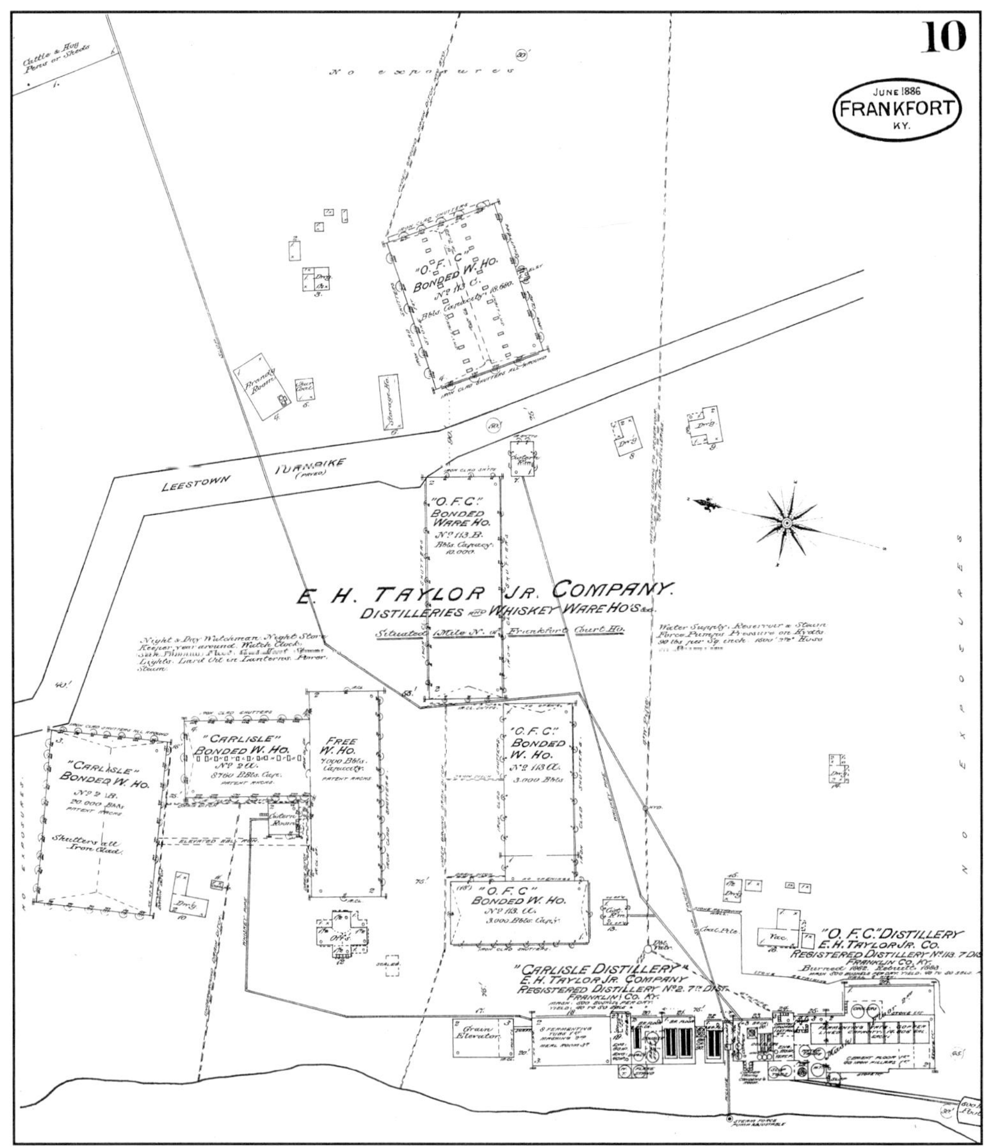

This map depicts the E. H. Taylor Jr. Co. in 1886. At the time, the company was comprised of the O. F. C. and Carlisle distilleries. Each of the operations had the capacity to produce 500 bushels of mash and 40 to 50 barrels of whiskey per day. Combined, the two distilleries had seven warehouses — enough space to store and age 70,440 barrels.

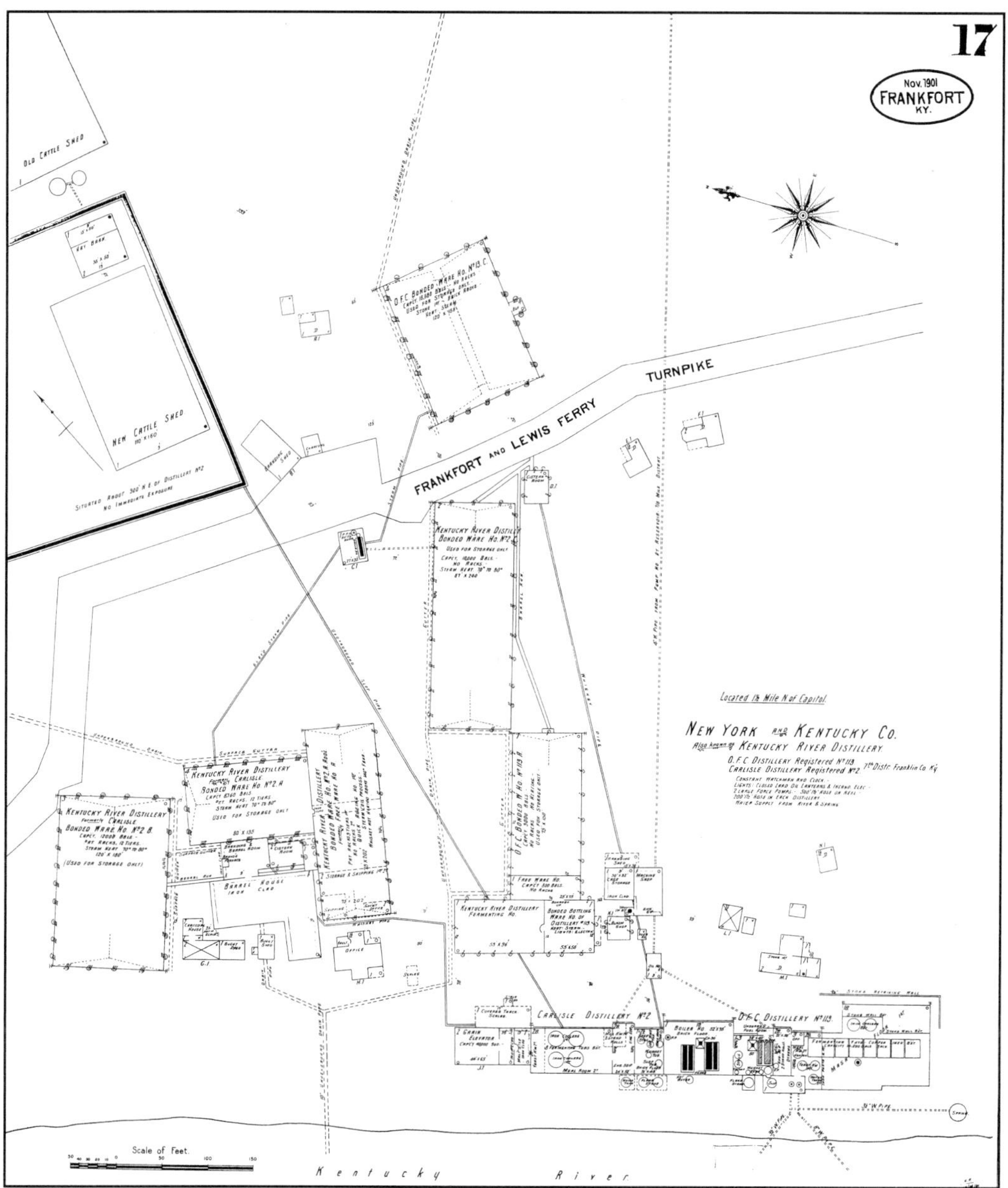

By 1901, the distillery had been renamed the Kentucky River Distillery, but was still comprised of the O. F. C. and the Carlisle distilleries. A centralized steam heating system had been added by this time, and Free Warehouse No. 2A had been converted into a bonded warehouse with a reduced capacity, used for "quick aging" experiments. Other additions included a new cattle shed (livestock were kept on the distillery grounds and fed the spent grain or slop from the fermenting process), branding shed, machine shop and case storage complex.

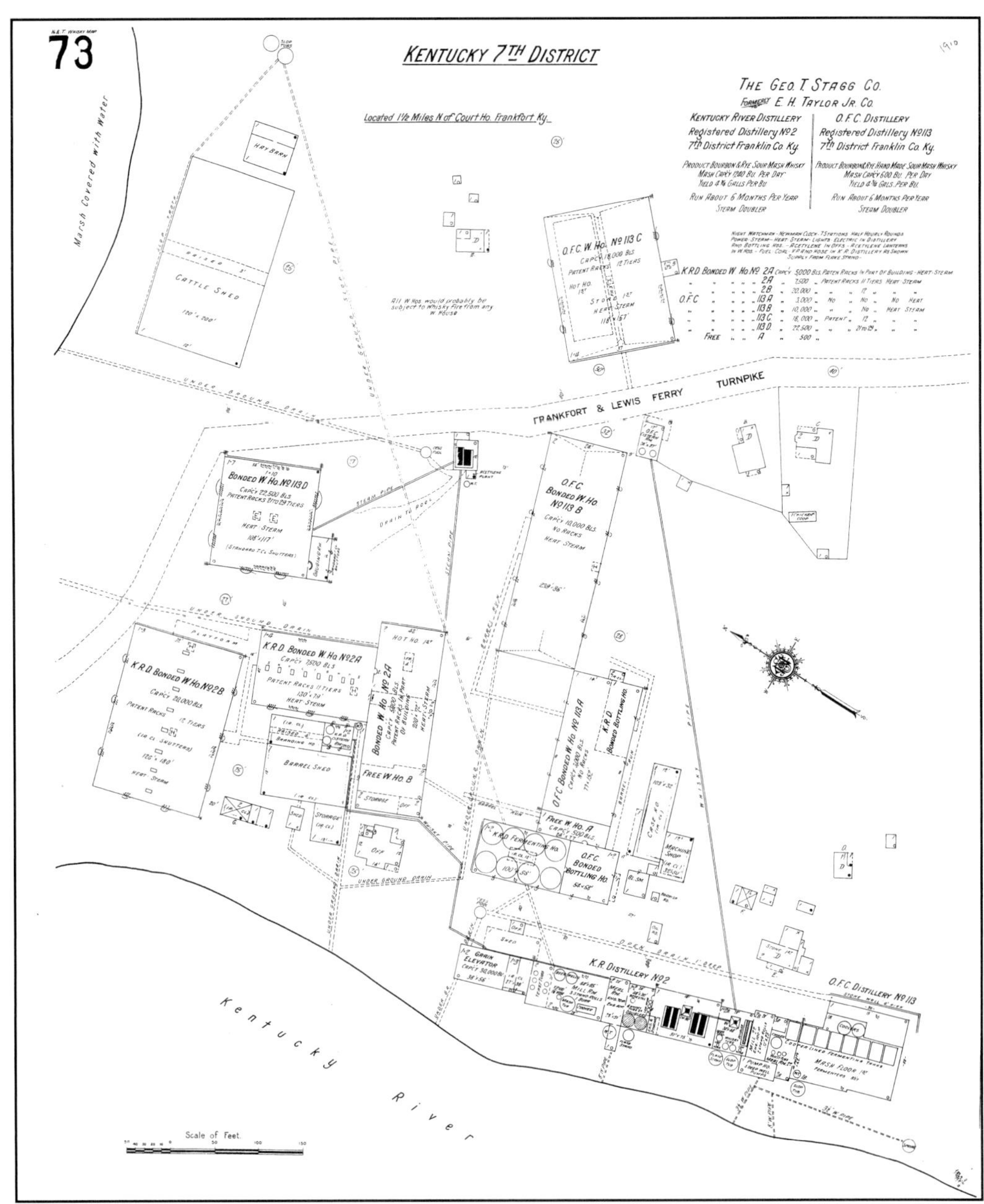

The Geo. T. Stagg Company owned the Kentucky River and O. F. C. distilleries by 1910. Electricity and acetylene lanterns had replaced lard oil lamps for lighting by this time. Production capacity for Kentucky River Distillery grew to 1,240 bushels of mash per day; the O. F. C. had a capacity of 600 bushels per day, 180 percent more than just 15 years earlier.

1868, that the growth and development of the distillery business in this country took an origin which has grown into its present magnitude and prosperity. It was then that the foresight, sagacity, and energy of Col. Edmund H. Taylor brought him to the front, and he became…a recognized leader in distillery construction, development and improvement.[4]

Active also in civic affairs, Taylor served as Frankfort's mayor for sixteen years between 1871 and 1887 until moving to "Thistleton," the home he built outside the city limits. Shortly after giving up the mayoral post, he was elected local state representative to the Kentucky General Assembly for the 1891-92 term. He was later elected to the state senate to complete the unexpired term of his predecessor, who had been sent to the U.S. Senate. When he completed his term, he was reelected to serve a full, four-year term, representing his district in the state senate.

One of his chief efforts was to promote the building of a new statehouse, an undertaking to which he applied considerable sums of his own money. U.S. Senator W. O. Bradley's Dedication Address for the new State Capitol on June 2, 1910, referred to the efforts of Louisville and Lexington to have the Capitol relocated:

> Despite the efforts to move it the determined citizens of this little city succeeded in keeping it. Among them Col. Edmund H. Taylor did the most effective work and to him the Frankfort people owe their chief debt of gratitude.[5]

In 1902, at age seventy-two, he also announced his candidacy for governor of the state, though for some reason, perhaps his advanced age, he dropped out before the election.

Well regarded, constantly in the public eye, Taylor became a Bluegrass institution, once described somewhat romantically as "last of the real colonels of the Bluegrass." Another family story illustrates the point. At one of the large dinner entertainments he held at "Thistleton," the wife of one of his guests, obviously not accustomed to the scale and luxury of the Colonel's hospitality, spilled a glass of red wine on the lace cloth of the elaborately set table. Recognizing her mortification, Colonel Taylor then almost instantly upset his own glass, feigning an accident but in fact sympathetically drawing attention away from her and relieving her embarrassment.

Before moving to "Thistleton," Taylor lived on the northeast corner of Main and Washington Streets in a mansion at the heart of the historic district of north Frankfort known as the "Corner in Celebrities." A large antebellum house (c. 1854), it now serves as offices for the Kentucky Heritage Commission, and most of its nineteenth-century character has been preserved. On West Main Street, a block or so from his home, he erected a fine, three-story Italianate building from which to oversee his many business interests. Built in the 1870s, the building now contains offices of the Franklin County Circuit Clerk.

Taylor liked to live and entertain on a large scale. One day, according to another family story, he asked his secretary to order him a carton of fine cigars. Mistaking "carton" for carload, the secretary placed the order, and in due time a boxcar of cigars arrived in Frankfort, what must have been hundreds of cartons containing tins of cigars. Good-humoredly, he kept them, either to spare her from embarrassment or because he knew in good time they would be consumed. His great-granddaughter proudly showed me one of the surviving tin boxes. The label read, "Humidor-packed, Chanticleer [brand name], Liberty Size, Ten Cigars."

Taylor also became a familiar personality in farming circles, celebrated for the Hereford cattle that he raised at Hereford Farms, his stock farm in adjoining Woodford County. An article in *The Breeders' Gazette* (1921) summed up his contributions as a stockbreeder: "...he has produced the kind of cattle that will make two pounds of beef grow where but one grew before."[6] He was equally well known for the hospitality that he dispensed at "Thistleton," his nine-hundred-acre estate a mile west from Frankfort on the Louisville Road (now Thistleton Heights subdivision). When he sumptuously entertained fifty-eight members of the American Association of

College Registrars at his farm in 1921, he was awarded a diploma that conferred on him the degree of "Master of Hospitality."

Until the reopening of Labrot & Graham Distillery in Woodford in 1996, Franklin was the only county in the Inner Bluegrass that continued to produce bourbon whiskey. The county remains the largest Bluegrass distiller of Kentucky bourbon, including Buffalo Trace. The two distilleries on Glenn's Creek — Old Taylor in Franklin and Old Crow in Woodford — have closed, though the Outer Bluegrass has several distilleries in Anderson County, including Wild Turkey and Four Roses on the Kentucky River. Besides several distilleries located in Daviess County, the largest concentration of bourbon distilleries is in the vicinity of Bardstown in Nelson County, which is located in the Outer Bluegrass.[7] Frankfort, on the fringe of the Inner Bluegrass, arguably became the center of whiskey-making in Central Kentucky. The destinies of E. H. Taylor, Jr., and Leestown were to meet at a time when the whiskey industry was undergoing change through modernization. Through a combination of experimentation and honoring the best traditions of whiskey-making, Taylor was to produce a whiskey of consistently high quality, a "hand-made" whiskey.[8]

Taylor's rise in the whiskey industry began at Leestown. In the years before the Civil War, changes elsewhere affected Leestown's future as a depot and trading center. The extension of the river trade farther north and the longer shipping season made possible by slack-water navigation left the warehouse at Leestown isolated and under-utilized. By 1840 it was no longer profitable as a place to store goods, and entrepreneurs began to realize its potential as an ideal setting for the production of whiskey, a use to which the site had been put on a small scale since early settlement. The advantages were obvious. Grain and other ingredients could be shipped in by river, the finished product shipped out. What was needed was individuals with resources and vision to capitalize on the potential of the site and its buildings.

In 1838 the Bank of Kentucky, which had acquired the warehouse and its four acres, sold the property for $600 to Jacob and Philip Swigert, two Frankfort businessmen. Owning other property locally, they decided to take on another partner, Thomas Theobold, forming Theobold, Swigert and Company, then acquiring additional property from landowner Harrison Blanton and other sellers in the Leestown vicinity. Daniel Swigert, Jacob's son, bought the Stony Point estate, which had belonged to Richard "Black Dick" Taylor, E. H. Taylor, Jr.'s, grandfather. In 1857 the company sold Jacob Swigert the property for one dollar. Referred to in the deed as "the Lees-town warehouse or pork house," the property for a time was apparently used as a facility for raising and processing swine. Realizing the commercial value of the property, Jacob Swigert converted the warehouse into a distillery, equipping it with a boiler that cost $1000, then a sizeable investment.

Swigert, who made improvements on the property to attract buyers, described it in an ad for its sale:

> This property is about one mile below Frankfort, and just below the Lock, and within the range of the proposed extension of navigation privileges. It has an excellent wharf, perfectly convenient for the landing of coal, wood, grain… and equally so for the shipment of everything either up or down the river. The improvements consist of a large three story stone warehouse, a still house, wood house, and excellent pens. The machinery is of the best and most approved patterns for making copper distilled Whisky… The establishment is supplied by a splendid spring of pure water which never fails and never gets muddy.[9]

Swigert's improvements enhanced the site considerably. The new boiler was steam-heated, an energy source that improved both the yield and the quality of distillation. Steam also powered the machinery that milled the grain and heated the beer to the boiling point much more effectively than the open wood fires used until that time. The stone warehouse was ideal for the aging of whiskey, and the wharf provided a means to ship the finished product to markets near and far. Because the whiskey industry controlled a sizeable volume of business, it had an influential voice in the river trade.

In fact, the whiskey industry dominated the freight trade on the Kentucky through much of the 1880s, though, as mentioned earlier, the river's main competitor, the railroad, slowly but steadily cut into its volume of transported freight.

The Leestown distillery was one of the first to be designed as a modern facility for the production of whiskey. Its capacity was greater, its production more efficient, its quality more uniform. Though improved techniques and more efficient hardware gradually developed from the earliest beginnings of commercial distilling in the eighteenth century, the Leestown distillery became a prototype for the "full-time, large-scale industrial distillery" that would set the standard for production after the Civil War.[10] It was a culmination of the industry's achievements, embodying the best techniques and distilling principles that had evolved by that time.

One factor that led to the emphasis on quality was simple economics. So-called "common" whiskey sold for very modest prices. On the New York market between 1858 and 1862 such whiskey sold wholesale for as little as 24 cents a gallon and even for less in Cincinnati, where it sold for 14 cents per gallon. This whiskey has been described as having a fresh, raw, corn taste, "a strong, objectionable taste and peculiar fiery flavor."[11] Much of it was "rectified" when it reached urban markets, meaning that it was "made pure" by one of two methods. The first was to pass it through a charcoal filter to leach out the harshness and then to add a burned sugar coloring "to smooth over its rankness and fieriness." The second, more elaborate method was to redistill the raw bourbon at high temperature as a means of removing the harsh secondary oils that gave it a raw taste. Then a smaller portion of unrefined bourbon was added "to restore bouquet, flavor, and the appearance of genuine whisky."[12]

Aged whiskey, on the other hand, had less of an edge, was smoother, mellower, and thus fetched a much higher price. As early as the 1830s, old whiskey sold for 25 cents a gallon and proportionately higher in the 1850s. This redistilled whiskey outsold the straight product at a ratio of fifteen to one. A better whiskey meant greater satisfaction among consumers and greater profit among producers, a formula that provided the motivation to produce the best bourbon possible. Taylor capitalized on the idea of producing a superior bourbon, his bottles bringing about twenty cents more per gallon.[13]

From the middle of the nineteenth century on, markets for Kentucky whiskey continued to expand, and the Kentucky River was a major artery in the river trade, the means by which barrels of whiskey were shipped to southern markets, especially New Orleans. The steamboat was a great boon to local distillers, who could inexpensively transport great quantities of liquid corn downriver. Though precise figures are hard to come by, it is documented that 21,298 barrels arrived at New Orleans in 1822.[14] By 1828 the number had doubled to more than 44,000 barrels. This amount translates into 880,000 cases, or 10,000,000 bottles. Railroads improved the distribution of whiskey as the country moved west, and whiskey emerged as the "ruby-hued comforter" that accompanied its settlement. Increased demand for quantities of whiskey caused the quality of whiskey generally to suffer. As adulterated and inferior whiskeys were produced to satisfy greater demand, the overall drop in quality created a niche for a product whose hallmark was quality. Among the many who competed to fill this niche was Edmund H. Taylor, Jr., who joined the ranks of the so-called "Bourbon Aristocrats."[15]

As mentioned earlier, Taylor had known Crow and associated with members of the Pepper family. He had successfully organized Gaines, Berry, and Company, one of the earliest and most distinguished whiskey agencies. He had learned the fundamentals at the established old-line distilleries along Glenn's Creek in adjacent Woodford County. In 1870, he sold off his interests in W. A. Gaines & Company, which owned the Old Crow Distillery and Hermitage Distillery in South Frankfort. With the $6,000 in assets he purchased a small existing distillery on the Leestown site from S. I. M. Major, Richard Tobin, and James Graham. The principal structures he purchased were the stone-and-frame building, the old Leestown warehouse, and "Riverside," the modest stone building on the other side of the lane that passed through the property and had belonged to his ancestor. Acquiring these facilities, he must have felt a sense of pride in returning to a place so rich in history associated with his family. "Riverside," the early stone-and-frame structure that came into his hands with the purchase, had been built, after all, by his great-grandfather.

The name he gave his newly acquired distillery was O.F.C., initials derived from "old fire copper," the distilling method that he adopted for use in the new plant. Immediately, he began to renovate the property and raise it to the highest standards of a state-of-the-art distillery. He bought new grinding machinery and massive columnar copper stills, then erected new buildings to house them. In 1872, he spent nearly 10 percent of the $250,000 total expended on construction in the whole of Franklin County. Investing $9,000 on substantial improvements at O.F.C., he also devoted $21,000 to altering the physical plant, demolishing the original building and replacing it with a larger and more modern structure.

Later company promotional material proudly touted all the improvements:

> Not a cent of expenditure has been withheld that could add a single detail to the completeness of the product, whether relating to the distinguishing properties of the whiskey, or the subsequent storage for speedy maturity.[16]

Through his capital investment and his attention to detail Taylor had demonstrated his commitment to producing a bourbon whiskey of unparalleled quality.

Throughout its long and sometimes adversarial relationship with the federal government, the whiskey industry underwent positive changes in response to new legislation. In the long run, many of these changes benefited and strengthened the industry. For example, a timely revision in the tax code under the U.S. Revenue Act of 1868 benefited distillers of fine whiskey in several ways. The increase in tax to fifty cents per proof gallon had the effect of driving up the price of whiskey and cutting down on the number of competing producers. The act required distillers to construct bonded warehouses. It also improved methods of collection and enforcement, which some illegal distillers had been able to avoid. It also authorized "detectives" to aid in the enforcement of its provisions, a first step in the ongoing war against illicit stills, many of which were situated in the hills and hollows of rural and eastern Kentucky. The act was applauded by legal distillers because it showed a resolve to collect excise taxes from the many illicit producers who competed unfairly with those who charged more to pay the tax imposed on what they produced.[17]

The Revenue Act opened another area of control that was to benefit both the industry and its consumers. It imposed requirements for labeling and identifying the contents of each barrel. Each was stamped with the date, serial number, and proof gallon contents as it went into the warehouse. When it came out, a second stamp was affixed, certifying the contents and that the tax had been paid. A stamped cask could not be re-used to sell any other spirit. The result was that aged straight whiskey could easily be distinguished from blended whiskey because the former was double-stamped, the latter single-stamped.

This legislation provided consumers with an early form of truth in packaging. The government was describing and certifying the contents of each barrel, distinguishing the quality straight whiskey (double-stamped) from the blended whiskey of lesser quality (single-stamped). The law also deferred the due date of tax payment to one year and eventually to three years. As a contemporary spokesman for the distillers stated before a Senate finance committee, the government stamps required to secure payment of the tax "gives to the distillers a trademark of great value, which more than compensates them for any inconvenience they suffer in raising money to pay the tax."[18] Less popular among distillers was the requirement that the distilleries pay the salaries of the two agents assigned to each plant. E. H. Taylor, Jr., never at a loss to turn a drawback to his advantage, used the presence of revenue agents in a novel way. He quoted them as experts, inserting testimonials and opinions in his promotional materials.

In its early stages, Taylor's business was successful enough that he expanded his operation beyond the Leestown property. Recruiting Lewis Castleman, a prosperous Frankfort resident, as a partner, the two investors purchased the Old Shield's Mill on Glenn's Creek, twelve miles south of Frankfort in Woodford County. Mostly with Castleman's capital and Taylor's knowledge, they rebuilt the mill, adapting it to the needs of a distillery and buying the necessary equipment. They named the distillery Glenn Spring. Eventually, relations became strained between the two over money and marketing of the product. Taylor sued Castleman when the latter stopped payment on a check. Castleman counterclaimed for breach of contract. Finally, Castleman ended the partnership by selling his portion of the distillery. Reasons for the breakup are not clear. One writer speculated that Taylor lost interest in the distillery because its product was not up to his high standards.[19] Always looking for opportunities, always ready to undertake a new venture, Taylor in 1874 went on to join James Pepper as a partner in the old Oscar Pepper distillery on Glenn's Creek.

Sometimes for better, sometimes for worse, Taylor's reach always exceeded his grasp. During this period Taylor's indebtedness began to outstrip his assets. A banker as much as he was a distiller, his method was to organize a distillery, finance it, and then sell off his interest to new investors and other companies. By the late 1870s, he was over-extended and could not meet all of his obligations. His relationship with The Frankfort and Lewis Ferry Turnpike Company is a case in point. Originally, he bought shares as a means of improving the road that wound around Rock Hill, through the distillery, and across Cove Spring Branch. The roadway was in desperate need of repair. When he paid for only part of the shares he had purchased, the paving company was eventually forced to sue for the balance. This incident was only a prelude to the problems he was soon to face with his O.F.C. Distillery.

Refitting the distillery had used up much of Taylor's financial resources. Taylor's strengths lay in renovation and operation, and sometimes his desire for creating the best exceeded his means. Not an on-the-road marketer, he was a master planner, preferring his office and the comforts of home to the rigors of constant travel, especially as he grew older. He was the person who created strategies and tactics, relying on others to take them to the marketplace. For this reason he contracted with Gregory, Stagg & Company, a

St. Louis commission firm, to sell and distribute his whiskey. When the pressure of his creditors became too great in 1877, he was forced to declare bankruptcy. George T. Stagg came to his rescue by paying off his creditors and consolidating many of his debts. To pay off his indebtedness to Stagg and his partner Clay Gregory, Taylor the next year had to sign over his distillery properties, including the O.F.C. distillery. Though they sold off most of Taylor's operations, Stagg and Gregory retained the O.F.C. distillery, apparently recognizing its earning potential. Coincidentally, the Pepper distillery on Glenn's Creek was sold to James Graham, the distiller from whom Taylor had purchased the O.F.C. distillery four years earlier in 1874.[20] Graham formed a partnership with Leopold Labrot, and together they set up the Labrot & Graham distillery at the site where its reincarnation recently resumed distilling.

During this period the distilling industry at Leestown acquired a new corporate neighbor. Hemp, as well as whiskey, has had a long and deep association with Leestown and the Bluegrass region. During most of the nineteenth century it was the major source of agricultural income for Kentucky farmers. Primarily used to make rope, sailcloth, and, later, bagging for cotton bales, hemp, according to the records, was stored at the Leestown warehouse and was among the items routinely shipped down the Kentucky.

The Kentucky River Mills at Leestown, the largest hemp mill in the state and one of the largest in the United States, was incorporated June 25, 1878. An earlier mill on the site had burned for a loss of $80,000. The new mill, located adjacent to Lock No. 4, was built at a cost of $12,000 with equipment valued at $50,000. Its purpose was to engage in "the manufacture of yarns, twines, clothes, and other fabrics from hemp, flax, and other fibers." It began by manufacturing yarn used in the backing of Brussels carpets. In a year or so the company switched to producing binder twine, accounting shortly for one-fourth of the binder twine produced in the United States. Drawing on the water power to drive a 72-inch turbine, the hemp factory, as it was referred to locally, was located immediately downstream from Lock No. 4 on the east side of the river at a site now occupied by Jim's Seafood restaurant, part of whose foundation is constructed from what remains of the laid-stone millrace along the river-bank.[21]

Among the original stockholders was Nathaniel S. Shaler (1841-1906), a native of Newport, Kentucky. Shaler was educated at Harvard as both botanist and zoologist, enlisting in the 5th Kentucky Volunteer Battery (Union) during the Civil War. For four years following the war, he taught paleontology at his alma mater, then served for a time as Kentucky State Geologist before returning to teach at Harvard as dean of Harvard's Lawrence Scientific School, a position he retained for the remainder of his life. In 1884 his *Kentucky: A Pioneer Commonwealth* was published. Preceded by Humphrey Marshall, Shaler became the second person associated with Leestown to write a history of Kentucky.

Leasing land from the state of Kentucky, Shaler and his fellow incorporators constructed a two-story, hemp-processing factory. Its dimensions were 54 feet by 210 feet. Not surprisingly, the building was constructed of stone quarried at the site. The original mill burned on October 6, 1883, and was rebuilt of brick in a one-story plan the next year. By the first decade of the twentieth century, Kentucky River Mills was one of the last hemp mills operating in the state. Cutting back and finally closing down when demand decreased in the late 1930s, it reopened during World War II to produce rope as well as marine oakum for the U.S. Navy. At its peak of production the plant employed 125 persons year around. It ceased operating in 1952, and the surviving structures of the disused mill complex were torn down during the early 1970s. For much of its history Leestown was as much associated with the hemp industry as it was with distilling.

As for the neighboring Leestown distillery not much farther than a stone's throw downriver, George Stagg, in full control by the late 1870s, launched his ambitious plans for expansion. He began to acquire adjoining property in the Leestown neighborhood, including a house and lot that was on the "avenue" laid out by Willis Lee nearly a hundred years earlier. This and purchases that followed marked the beginning of the enlargement of the distillery property. Located on a relatively small parcel of land, the distillery would eventually include all of the section of Leestown known as Taylortown. Then, it was an expanse of fields with a scattering of frame and stone houses extending to the Frankfort and Lewis Ferry Road that ran along the base of a hill to the northeast and crossing Cove Spring Branch. The distillery and its grounds were expanding close to its present size of 110 acres.

Joining with E. H. Taylor, Jr., and a St. Louis associate named Gustave Boeffler, George Stagg incorporated as E. H. Taylor, Jr., Company, wisely retaining Taylor's name, which had become identified with the production of high-quality bourbon whiskey. In addition to purchasing, building, and leasing whiskey distilleries and warehouses as well as the production, purchase, and sale of whiskey, the Stagg company also dealt in livestock. Distillers commonly kept stock on the distillery grounds, feeding it with a protein-rich slop, one of the by-products of distillation. This efficient but unaesthetic operation provided a profitable use for what otherwise would be an expense, and many other distilleries followed the practice. It would be some years before distilleries perfected a means to dry the slop and ship it elsewhere to feed someone else's cattle and hogs. When the transition was made, the cleanliness of the grounds and the quality of the overall environment must have improved measurably.

A new firm, Stagg, Hume, and Co., formed to bottle and distribute the whiskey produced at O. F. C. distillery. William Hume represented the firm in St. Louis, Taylor ran the Leestown distillery, and Stagg did much of the traveling necessary to promote their interests.

Though the relationship among the parties was sometimes uneasy, the company prospered, declaring its first dividend in August 1881, in the amount of $273,843.34. Building on its successes, the company opened a second distillery at Leestown between 1879 and 1880. This new facility was named Carlisle, for John G. Carlisle, a U.S. congressman from Kentucky — and a future Speaker of the House — who had been active as an advocate for the whiskey industry. Carlisle was instrumental in passing legislation (1879) extending the bonding period from one to three years and exempting whiskey lost through leakage, evaporation, and related causes from taxation. When the barreled whiskey was withdrawn from the bonded warehouse, the government's gauger remeasured the amount of whiskey in each barrel, determining the amount of *outage* — thus saving the distillery from paying taxes, within prescribed limits, on non-existent whiskey.[22]

For its first several years, the E. H. Taylor, Jr., Distillery prospered, but for whatever reasons the corporation was dissolved in 1884 and its stock reissued. Taylor possessed a one-third interest in the company, an interest he had purchased mostly on credit. Hume went on to open his own distillery, though he kept some association with the O. F. C. distillery. Following the continuity of relationships that the Leestown facility fostered, a Hume was working at the distillery as late as 1916.[23]

In the fall of 1881 the industry faced another problem as whiskey prices depreciated in response to a cut in the rates at which it was taxed. This created pressure for producers to lower their prices and for competitors to make whiskey deals at more attractive prices. To the extent they could, many buyers backed out of their futures contracts to buy whiskey. The result was an overstock of whiskey in distillers' warehouses, and overproduction invariably produced a glut on the market and less profitable returns.[24] This setback hastened efforts during the 1880s to search for new markets abroad, especially in Europe. It also presented a means to evade the internal revenue tax on whiskey removed from bonded warehouses, since whiskey destined for foreign markets was exempted from the tax.

These forces did not seem to strain the resources of Taylor and Stagg because in the fall of 1882 the company expanded again, purchasing a company on the Versailles and McCracken's Mill Turnpike in Woodford County. This brought to three the number of distilleries that the company owned. The newly acquired distillery was located on a site of a small distillery that had operated since 1816, making it one of the prototypes for producing whiskey in a county that had played a central role in the evolution of whiskey-making. The seller was Jacob Swigert Taylor, E. H. Taylor, Jr.'s, son, who had purchased the property three years before and had made substantial improvements on it. Another generation of Taylors had made its debut in the distilling industry.

69

The exuberant mood of expansion and a promising future for the Leestown distilleries were dealt a sobering blow by natural forces. During that same year lightning struck the flagship O.F.C. distillery at Leestown and burned it to the ground. The cost of rebuilding was $44,762.58 over and above what was covered by insurance.[25] Though such occurrences were rare, they tended, when they came, to be devastating. Fearing fire and destruction by other natural causes, most distillers paid hefty premiums to insure against them. This was the age before sprinkler systems, high-volume water pumping capability, and mobile fire trucks. Though fires were relatively infrequent, Taylor and Stagg must have remembered the 1862 warehouse fire in Frankfort that destroyed 4,500 barrels of whiskey and set the river afire, much in the same manner as the conflagration on the Kentucky River in Anderson County at Wild Turkey Distillery in the spring of 2000.

V.

The Pure Product & Its Producer

Though he was not always a provident money manager, E. H. Taylor, Jr., was recognized as the maker of first-rate bourbon whiskey in "the old-fashioned, hand-made, sour mash, fire copper method." This time-proven process, which was standard practice in the pioneer distilleries to which he was linked, produced the best results. First, the grain was mashed and mixed by hand. Then it was fermented in small wooden tubs no larger than a barrel. Sometimes the same tubs served both for mashing and fermentation. Fresh yeast was used only at the start. After three mashes, the spent distillate, or sour mash, was used to start fermentation. The result was a unique consistency in the final product. The fermented mixture, referred to as beer, was distilled twice in copper vessels over open wood fires. Though stills grew larger as the industry adapted to growing demand during the 1870s, copper or copper plating became a fixed feature in the distilling process.[1]

The process was embodied in the very name O. F. C. (Old Fire Copper whiskey) and was adapted to the gilded age of industrial expansion with three-story continuous stills; enormous reinforced, brick warehouses; and expansive grounds. Changing the scale of production in some instances meant sacrificing the quality of the final product. Though elsewhere many compromises were made in the interest of increasing production and profits, the small distillery at Leestown remained one of a half-dozen or so that continued to produce whiskey following established traditions. A roving correspondent for the *New York World,* writing in 1872, noted the distinction between those who professed to make the genuine product and those who actually did:

> The number of distilleries claiming to produce the real old bourbon, the pure, unadulterated "handmade sour-mash old fashioned copper" is more than I could enumerate, but the number that actually do make the purest bourbon is very easily computed.[2]

Writing under the sobriquet *Rolling Stone,* this correspondent spent two months in Kentucky visiting distilleries, finding only three that still produced whiskey in the old way. The one that impressed him most was the small distillery at Leestown. Significantly, Taylor the next year professed to be the only sour mash whiskey maker in Kentucky who distilled his whiskey in copper over an open wood fire. One testament to his farsightedness was the fact that he was imitated by other distillers, who recognized the advertising advantages of claiming to produce quality whiskey through the hand-made, open-fired, copper method. Trade journals of the day contained ads claiming that given whiskeys were "hand-made," "fire copper," and "small-tub." [3]

Despite these claims, old-time distillers like Taylor, discriminating and proud, discounted many of their rivals' claims as false:

> Thousands of barrels yearly go on the market and are sold with no other belief in the buyer than that he is handling or consuming a hand-made sour mash whiskey, when, in fact, it is only a grade of machine goods, distilled by an artificial process, of inferior materials, by inferior appliances, and deleterious both to health and morals.[4]

Though Taylor's condemnation may seem unduly harsh, it's true that few distillers in Kentucky possessed the quality of physical plant and appliances used at Leestown's O.F.C. and Carlisle distilleries.

The process by which Taylor and his successors made whiskey at O.F.C. was painstaking and distinctive. First, the grain was milled to a coarse flour in the mill room. Originally, during the 1870s when the distillery produced about ten barrels a day, Taylor grew his own corn on the hills adjacent to the distillery. As the volume of production increased, corn had to be brought in from outside. Close attention to every detail of manufacture contributed to the quality of the final product. In addition to using the best obtainable ingredients, the method of production contributed to his whiskey's superiority. The formula that he used for his mash was richer and more expensive, the grain being ground by two separate corrugated rollers, an improvement over the older method of grinding the grain with mill stones, a process that was uneven and pulverized the grain. Taylor preferred to use the corrugated rollers, which broke the grain and created a uniform mass better suited for fermentation.[5]

When the grain was reduced to granules, the next step was to cook the flour with sour beer saved from a previous run. Here Taylor used a patented technique, which he had helped devise during the 1870s. The effect was to improve the sour beer, a critical factor, Taylor believed, in creating his superior bourbon. The effect of this "strained-slop process" was to filter out the "dead" meal and create a "rich creamy liquid" instead of an "inert mass," which competitors used to cook their mash. In his words, "properly handled by the skilled distiller, the use of this strained spent beer is a valuable aid in the attainment of a faultless fermentation." [6] A further advantage of this process, which did not go unnoticed, was that it produced almost a gallon more of whiskey per bushel of grain.

Next, the mash was cooked to a temperature of about 112 degrees, then permitted to cool. After it had cooled sufficiently, workers known as "mash hands" stirred the mixture with paddles called "mash sticks." At this stage of the process "virgin" water from the historic spring was added, drawn from a holding pool and pumped into the distillery. As in pioneer days, the tubs in which the mashing was performed were small, no larger than a bushel. The intense labor that was required raised the price of whiskey by five or ten cents a gallon.[7] What made the extra expense justifiable was the superior taste that resulted from this method.

The O. F. C. distillery produced bourbon in the hand-mashed way; the neighboring Carlisle distillery mashed its whiskey by machine. On the second floor of the O. F. C. in a room that was 10,000 square feet, a hundred or more mash tubs were lined up, and a crew of two dozen or more men hand-worked the mash with their mash sticks. The modern alternative was next door in the form of power-driven rakes, which worked the mash in enormous tubs.

In the fermenting room beneath the mash room, Taylor substituted copper vats for the wooden tubs that had been used in the past. Copper was easier to clean. Residues and filth that collected in and around the wooden tubs were neutralized in the almost antiseptic glitter of the copper vats whose surfaces lent themselves to thorough cleaning. The fermenting room contained eight such vats, each with a capacity exceeding 14,000 gallons. Their bases were set six inches into a floor of high-grade limestone, which was sealed with English cement, their sides rising to within eleven feet of the elevated ceiling.

The design of the work space reflected the latest thinking and most recent innovations. Mash, for example, was moved from one floor to the other with pumps. Numerous windows provided both ventilation and light, creating a healthful and pleasant environment for work. Important, too, was using "top quality" yeast, which was introduced to a new tub of mash from one already fermented. Taylor claimed that this method, long employed in the traditional procedures of sour-mash whiskey-making, ensured a whiskey "free from the contaminations of acids and chemicals imparted by the use of many artificial yeasts… to which medical men attribute diseases unknown when only the old-fashioned Copper Whiskeys were drunk."[8] Taylor followed a "96-hour plan" in his process of fermentation.

As the industry elsewhere modernized by switching to machinery that altered the method of producing hand-made, sour mash whiskey, Carlisle and O.F.C. continued to follow the practice of mashing by hand. They persistently continued to follow the traditional methods well into the 1930s, while virtually every other distillery had mechanized the process long before. Taylor did depart from tradition in using larger fermentation vats. His reason was that it was more difficult to maintain an even temperature in the smaller vats. The large copper vats that he preferred produced a mash that was more consistent and uniform in its fermentation. He regarded using them as "one of the most indispensable steps in the process of making a perfect whiskey." As many visitors and experts in the industry commented, Taylor was almost unique in using copper vats. From the time the grain was ground until the time it was barreled, Taylor's whiskey came into contact only with copper.

Taylor also took pride in the barrels in which his whiskey "slept." Very likely using coopers employed by the company, he had barrels made at the distillery, many of them from the stand of white oaks on a part of the distillery grounds. When production increased, he necessarily had to purchase barrels beyond the premises. During the 1880s many of these were supplied from the great oak forests of the North. When these sources were depleted in the 1890s, he had to rely on southern oak, which was more porous and "loose-fibered." [9] To offset increased leakage and evaporation, he enlarged the barrels from a capacity of forty to forty-eight gallons.

Barreled, the whiskey was "put to bed," first in the old Leestown warehouse perched on the bank of the river, later in the newly designed warehouses of the O.F.C. and Carlisle distilleries. Set back some distance from the river, these contained three tiers. In 1882 the old warehouse, better suited to production, was displaced by these newer warehouses, which were drier and uniformly warm — the best conditions for proper aging. Each floor, or tier, held three vertical rows of barrels. This three-tier system made the best use of light, ventilation, and dryness. Natural conditions were supplemented by a steam heating system. Painstaking and fastidiously applied, these procedures produced a whiskey in which the company took great pride:

It is a known fact and subject of much comment with the revenue officers that the whiskeys of this company are of higher proof and are more uniform in color, temperature, and quality than any whiskeys of the same age in the country.[10]

In addition to adhering to strictly observed methods of production, Taylor had the knack of promoting his product energetically and cleverly. From the beginning, hospitality was his hallmark. He was the prototype for a "Colonel" Harland Sanders, but in addition to the image he was the genuine article without the hokum. In a time when visitors to distilleries were greeted with no-admittance signs, he welcomed the public to view his distilling rooms. As proud of his distilling facilities as he was of the product, he recognized the value of opening his doors to show that he had no secrets and that his whiskey was made according to the time-tried and painstaking "old way."

Not content to wait for the world to come to the distillery and sample his product, he invited prominent citizens to inspect the distilling process in all phases of production. For example, in 1873 he sent a barrel of whiskey to Jeffrey Alexander, president of the Lexington Gas Company, inviting him to tour the O.F.C. when he came to Frankfort. Taylor also excelled in gaining endorsements from such individuals and entities as the governor of Kentucky, Farmers Bank, and the Bank of Kentucky. But this was not the only means Taylor used to promote his product. A family tradition, verified by a clipping in a family scrapbook, relates that when Taylor began to market whiskey with his own name on the label he had eight freight cars full of empty bottles sent to New York. Each bottle contained his distinctive E.H. Taylor label. He hired "distributors" to place his empty bottles around restaurants, clubs, and hotels. As a result, by the time his whiskey went on the market, buyers were familiar with the name. As the writer of the article noted, buyers were "softened up" when the Old Taylor salesmen called.[11]

A recent biographical sketch of Colonel E.H. Taylor, Jr., summarized Taylor's career as the "father of the modern bourbon industry:"

He started or operated at least seven different distilleries in his career, pioneered modern "brand marketing" in the sale of his whiskeys, and fought tirelessly for federal government protection of straight bourbon whiskey." [12]

What his forebears possessed in martial aggressiveness came down to E. H. Taylor, Jr., in the form of a militant insistence on preserving the integrity of the whiskey he produced. Having the good fortune to be born at a critical time in the development of the distilling industry, he followed a career that bridged the "classic and modern eras" of bourbon making, a bridge that he in large part contributed to build.

After Taylor left the Leestown distilleries, George T. Stagg continued the active promotion of its whiskeys with illustrated promotional pamphlets and other publications. One commentator, noting the distillery's "open door policy," attributed the lack of secrecy in production to the quality of production: "The very fact that it is the true old way, and that there is no patent secret attached, is what gives them liberty to make strangers welcome." [13] Under Stagg promotional efforts continued in the form of printed pamphlets describing its whiskeys as "liquid velvet," "the only whisky for the home side-board, the club restaurant, the hotel cafe, and the medicine chest…and only high class dealers sell it." [14]

Few competitors could match the impressiveness of the physical plant. One of the warehouses, built in 1907, was singled out by a prominent local architect. In noting the durability of its thick brick walls and the sturdiness of its interior rick frames, he praised it as the "fine individual building" in the complex and "a national standard of whiskey warehouse construction." [15] Built earlier, the two other warehouses are similarly well constructed.

After its reconstruction in 1883, the main distillery building was 212 feet long and 56 feet wide. Two stories high with an imposing spired tower, it was sectioned off by massive stone walls into large chambers containing meal and mill rooms, a boiler room, and a still room. Its two-story addition, still standing, was built into the sloping river bank with a mash floor on the upper level and a fermenting room below. Though lacking a tower, the neighboring Carlisle facility was built along similar though smaller-proportioned lines. Architecturally, both plants in their day were models of modern, industrial construction, solidly built structures exemplifying the principle of form following function. As with their counterparts from the earliest days of whiskey-making, all phases of the distilling process were housed under a single roof—from raw grain and water to finished product. The only real difference was scale.

During the 1880s whiskey produced at Leestown found its way to the world markets in Europe and elsewhere, in part as a means of avoiding the internal revenue tax but also as a hopeful attempt to expand the market for Kentucky bourbon. An import/export firm in New York, for example, had 180 barrels of its Carlisle whiskey housed at its facility in Bremen, Germany.[16]

As the unofficial spokesman for the industry, Taylor chided the U.S. Congress for its failure to aid the industry in finding a solution for the overproduction and surplus of whiskey on the market, a surplus that seriously threatened the industry's long-term economic health. The vehicle for sending this message was a *New York Times* interview in August 1885. During the summer of the next year, he helped form a syndicate which proposed to buy whiskey on the market that had been produced between 1779 and 1873. The proposal died a natural death, perhaps because the syndicate lacked the funds to purchase the whiskey it identified, estimated to be at least 77,000 barrels in addition to the whiskey that they themselves had produced.[17]

As the fortunes of the Leestown distilleries rose, for a time Taylor's flagged. These were not prosperous years for E. H. Taylor, Jr., personally as his financial interest in the company that bore his name steadily eroded. Though in 1884 he was listed as the company's vice-president under its president, George T. Stagg, he in fact owned only a nominal one share in company stock when it was reissued in 1884. The real power and direction of the company was controlled by Stagg, who owned 2,498 of the company's 2,500 shares. Taylor was still beset with financial troubles in the wake of his bankruptcy in 1877. To add insult to injury, the company's fancy buggy, painted black and its running gear trimmed out in red, was mistakenly sold at a sheriff's auction to satisfy claims under his previous bankruptcy.[18]

As Stagg transferred shares of stock to New York investors, Taylor increasingly felt inclined to disassociate himself and his name from the company. He requested Stagg to enter an agreement of some kind to end his connection with E. H. Taylor, Jr., Company, Distillers. Under the agreement reached near the end of 1886, the company's Woodford County plant went to Taylor and sons in consideration of releasing his interest in the company that bore his name. Allegedly, there was an oral promise to change the company name. One of Taylor's three sons, Jacob Swigert Taylor (b. 1853), was a witness to the agreement between his father, Stagg, and George Watson, the firm's accountant. He described it as "a casual affair." The meeting occurred on New Year's Day of 1887 and was later to be the subject of much contention and debate.[19]

Stagg went on to reorganize the George T. Stagg Company and moved its headquarters to Louisville, Kentucky. Soon after, the E. H. Taylor, Jr., Company for several months conveyed its Leestown distilleries to the Louisville firm before reconveying them to the parent company and retaining the Taylor name for the duration of its charter. The one thing that remained constant through this process, starting in 1880, was the E. H. Taylor name in a facsimile of Taylor's signature beneath the label, both on the O. F. C. and Carlisle brands. Because one's signature could be protected under the laws against forgery, a signature on each label offered some protection against counterfeiters. Taylor borrowed the idea of identifying his whiskey in script from some packages of imported brandy that he saw in St. Louis. Experimenting, he found that his autograph on barrels and bottles made a distinctive and personalized trademark. Whatever his skills with finances, Taylor was undeniably a great merchandiser, having an instinct for sales that carried him and the companies to prosperity.

In the distillery he now owned on Glenn's Creek, Taylor also used his signature, branding each barrel with a similar mark. Not wishing for George T. Stagg and Company to profit from his good name and his distinctive mark, early in 1889 he demanded that the company cease using his autograph on its products since he was no longer associated with it and did not wish the company to profit from his name.[20] When Stagg and Company ignored his request, he went to court. The outcome, not finally adjudicated until two years later, was an injunction from the county court preventing E. H. Taylor, Jr., Company from using E. H. Taylor, Jr.'s signature and his name as a brand name, or from promoting their products as having been produced by the individual that people identified with the name of E. H. Taylor, Jr. George T. Stagg and Company was required to remove Taylor's name from all whiskey produced since Taylor's departure from the company. In later life, Albert Blanton remembered as a child of ten seeing workers laboring to erase the Taylor name and relettering the warehoused barrels at the distillery.

But Taylor's problems weren't over. Though Stagg and Company erased the Taylor mark from its products as required, it continued to operate under the name E. H. Taylor, Jr., Company. Worse, from Taylor's point of view, early in 1890 it moved its company headquarters back to Leestown. Oddly and uncomfortably for both, the companies maintained separate offices in the same building on the distillery property. Though they were competitors now, Stagg continued to use the Taylor name on its products. To further himself, in 1894 Taylor organized a new firm called E. H. Taylor, Jr., & Sons. This, of course, rankled those operating under the name E. H. Taylor, Jr., Company, since the names were identical in the minds of most people. The proximity of separate businesses with virtually identical names must have caused considerable confusion inside and outside the company offices.

When Taylor sued in Franklin County Circuit Court to have the company's name changed on grounds that it had ceased to exist in 1887, the court ruled in his favor, only to be reversed on appeal. The high court's opinion permitted the company to continue doing business as E. H. Taylor, Jr., Company. Taylor himself seemed to have accepted this verdict, for admittedly he did business with the company after leaving it. One of the reasons weakening Taylor's case at law was the fact that there was no contract stipulating the dissolution of the E. H. Taylor, Jr., Company. One can imagine Taylor, regarded by himself and others as a gentleman, being content, at least then, to reach agreements on the strength of his personal word without the legal apparatus of a written contract. In the end, Taylor had not proved that George T. Stagg had dissolved the old company in establishing a new one and locating its office, for a time, in Louisville. Though Taylor anticipated the imminent failure of the company because of its high costs of operation and its substantial debt, the E. H. Taylor, Jr., Company in fact continued operating under its corporate name until 1904.[21]

During the testimony, Taylor's reputation as a "practical" distiller was contested. George Watson of the Stagg Company alleged that Taylor had no special knowledge of distilling and that his efforts lay largely in handling office paperwork. For his part, Taylor testified that though he did not physically undertake the steps necessary to ferment and distill whiskey, he did personally oversee each step of the operation and had intimate knowledge of the process in every phase.

Understandably, Taylor began to redirect his energies toward the Glenn's Creek distillery that came to him in 1887 as part of his severance from the E. H. Taylor, Jr., Company. Stagg additionally agreed to lend Taylor $10,000 to get the distillery started. At the time of the transaction Taylor also bought 1,200 barrels of whiskey that had been distilled at the Glenn's Creek plant, an asset that he used to finance his start-up costs. He was anxious to see his new company succeed and saw it as a future triumph over his Leestown competitor.

Though Taylor had predicted the imminent failure of the Leestown facility, reports of its demise, to paraphrase Mark Twain, were greatly exaggerated. In 1889, for example, the E. H. Taylor, Jr., Company at Leestown produced profits of $125,000. Both Taylor and the E. H. Taylor, Jr., Company had made a sizeable investment in the physical plant of the Leestown property, creating a state-of-the-art distillery complex that must have daunted competitors. The O.F.C. and Carlisle distilleries extended across most of the Leestown plateau and invariably impressed those who saw it. "No language that we can use in a brief business report will do it justice," one outside expert observed, "…[I]t is the ne plus ultra of its class." A revenue agent, D. W. Voyles, described it as "perfect and admirable." [22] Another tribute to the quality of his product is that it was said his whiskey brought twenty cents more per gallon than other whiskeys, a price most consumers were willing to pay for whiskey with which his name was associated.

As for E. H. Taylor, Jr., his financial ups and downs continued well into the next century. Increasingly in his later years, his civic activities as mayor and his business activities made him a popular and well-known figure in the Bluegrass and beyond. In 1871 he was elected mayor of Frankfort for the first of continuous two-year terms that lasted sixteen years. By any measure he had a significant role in Frankfort's two major industries — government and bourbon-making. When he moved to "Thistleton," his estate outside the city limits, he was no longer eligible to run for mayor.

Undeterred, Taylor ran first for state representative and then for state senator, being elected to both offices. During the time he served in the senate, his personal fortunes diminished as his personal expenses and commitments mounted. One of them was money spent in thwarting yet another effort to move the capital from Frankfort to Louisville or Lexington. His skills as a tactician, however, never flagged. When an appropriation bill for a new capitol was defeated, Taylor adroitly revived and passed it (in a move described as a "bombshell") by attaching it to a revenue bill. A man of great vigor, he must have also been something of a juggler, for during most of his political career he also played an active role in the bourbon and stock-raising businesses. There is a family story that at the turn of the century when he was about seventy, he lay ill — at death's door, his family thought at the time. As two of his doctors were leaving his sickroom, one of them commented that it was a pity that someone who had done so much in his life should "die poor." The Colonel's eyes were said to have popped open determinedly. Soon he recovered, living another twenty-three years and dying, in fact, a wealthy man with an estate valued in 1923 at $2.5 million. [23]

By 1886, when he was serving his final term as Frankfort's mayor, he turned his attention to his last great whiskey endeavor, building the only distillery that would bear his name. Occupying 136 acres on Glenn's Creek in a narrow valley near Millville in Franklin County, this distillery, disused but still substantially intact, was a showplace out of the novels of Sir Walter Scott. Built on the site of the 1879 Jacob Swigert Taylor distillery, it resembled a medieval castle with turrets, towers, and crenelated walls. Adjacent to the Old Crow distillery, the property was elaborately landscaped with gardens, pools, gazebos, and miniature bridges. All three of his sons — Edmund, Jacob Swigert, and Kenner — joined him in the whiskey business. The Old Taylor distillery operated nearly thirty years until it fell victim to Prohibition. One of the family tales probably relates to this period. According to one account, Colonel Taylor went to New York to try to sell his last distillery. To make a positive impression, he was decked out in one of his tailored linen suits and was wearing a diamond stick through his tie. What the prospective buyers could not see was the hole in the seat of his pants. The teller then averred that the incident epitomized Colonel Taylor: he had a bravura "front," at times with not much more than gumption behind it.[24]

In later years, increasingly relying on his sons to manage his whiskey interests, he concentrated his attention on breeding prize livestock. At the Bluegrass Fair in 1914 one of his bulls won three prizes. In 1921 at the International Livestock Show, his champion Hereford steer, Woodford Marvel, won an award in the classification of "fat cattle." The grand old man of the whiskey industry gradually retired from business pursuits to spend time with his family and enjoy his country estate, dying in 1923 at age ninety-two.

An article in the *Frankfort State Journal* glowingly assessed his contributions to the whiskey industry, describing him as "an early example of the professional executive," able to project himself into all phases of the business — production, finance, sales promotion — always insisting on "pure goods." The same article best summarizes the importance of his contributions to the whiskey industry: "Taylor has been described as perhaps the most remarkable man to enter the whiskey industry during the post–Civil War years."

VI.

Toward the New Century

The leestown distilleries by the mid-1880s were not only extensive and handsome but productive. The combined daily mash capacity in 1890 was 1,000 bushels, which produced a yield of 80 to 100 barrels of what came to be described as "Kentucky's finest, hand-made sour mash bourbon whiskey." [1] The site occupied twenty acres. Among four bonded warehouses and two so-called "free" warehouses the capacity for storage was over 70,000 barrels. To show the difference in capacity and output, E. H. Taylor's distillery on Glenn's Creek had a warehousing capacity of only 8,000 barrels.

Seeking additional capital, George Stagg entered a business agreement with Walter B. Duffy of Rochester, New York. Duffy, who owned his own distillery in Rochester, produced a medicinal liquor whose major ingredient was whiskey. Manufacturing essentially a patent medicine, he advertised it as a nostrum for a variety of medical ills, attempting to escape a whiskey tax. In 1885 Duffy leased the Carlisle distillery at Leestown and produced about 850 barrels of whiskey.

As the relationship developed, Duffy invested $75,000 in the Stagg Company and gained increasing control over it and its subsidiary at Leestown. During the last decade of the century Stagg slowly divested himself of the company's stock. By 1895 Duffy and his associates were officers in the company, and by the turn of the century owned nearly all of its stock. W.J. Naylon, president of the Erie Distillery of Buffalo, New York, became treasurer of the distillery in that year, the same year that W.B. Duffy became its vice-president. The Duffy and Naylon families (originally associates of Duffy) were to control the distilleries for the better part of the next three decades until the waning years of Prohibition, when they were acquired by Schenley Distillery.[2]

Under new ownership, the E.H. Taylor, Jr., Company distilleries underwent some upgrading. The Carlisle distillery was remodeled and renamed the Kentucky River Distillery. This was in part to permit the introduction of a new and "cheaper" whiskey to supply "a large demand for goods of a lower grade than either O.F.C. or Carlisle," two brands of straight Kentucky whiskey whose reputation and quality no one dared to compromise. During 1899 the O.F.C. and general plant area were improved by an investment of $65,000. One of the improvements was a cooperage, which permitted the plant to resume making its own barrels. Another was a bottling house which could bottle over 150 cases each day. New cattle pens and appropriate sheds were built on the northeast corner of the property, increasing the capacity to 1,200 or 1,300 head.

The new owners next took initiatives to consolidate their Kentucky and New York holdings under a trust or "combine" called the New York and Kentucky Company. The George T. Stagg Company and the E.H. Taylor, Jr., Company and the Kentucky River Distillery made up the Bluegrass segment of the company's eight subsidiaries. Covering the whole spectrum of whiskey-making— with the Kentucky holdings substantially representing the top-of-the-line, sour mash whiskey — it was in a position to prosper. Additionally, its Kentucky distilleries also put out a lesser-grade "contract whiskey," and at the low end the out-of-state distilleries produced a malt whiskey for use "medicinally" and billed as an "absolutely pure and healthful tonic" that could be applied to treat malaria.[3] As measured by capital and production, the New York and Kentucky Company was the third-largest of the combines that formed in the last two decades of the nineteenth century. Part of their purpose was to control the excessive amount of whiskey that was producing a glut in the marketplace. As might be expected, E.H.Taylor, Jr., sent out notice that neither he nor E.H. Taylor, Jr., & Sons had any connection with the newly formed trust. At the beginning of 1900 the company made its first public stock offering. By the turn of the century the distilleries at Leestown were competitive and productive in the growing whiskey market both at home and abroad.

During the next century whiskey-making on the site was to continue and evolve in new ways under new owners, surviving Prohibition and other governmental regulation as well as changing tastes and preferences of whiskey consumers. There came a host of economic, political, and social challenges to the industry that would have been unimaginable to James Crow, the Peppers, and E.H. Taylor, Jr. For decades after 1881, the problem of over-production affected the economic health of the whiskey industry. Sales at the Leestown distilleries continued briskly during the 1880s, as name recognition, overall quality of product, and the efficiency of the facilities all contributed to the prosperity. As over-production became a problem in the industry, the Leestown distilleries often would buy back over-stocks of its whiskeys, knowing that additional aging would increase its value and marketability. Salesmen and drummers were employed to take orders for the whiskey in new markets.

Known first as "commercial travelers," these roadmen were a colorful group. George P. Mills, an aggressive sales rep for George T. Stagg, was typical, as an anecdote printed in the trade publication *The Wine and Spirit Bulletin* indicates:

We had gone into a well-known resort to indulge in a little Kentucky straight. There was a new bartender on. We asked for a little whisky, and they handed out the regular bar bottle of blended goods. George said, "Say, young fellow, you have O.F.C., have you not?" "Oh, yes," said the mixer of drinks. "We keep it all the time." "That's just the trouble," said Mills, "I don't want you to keep it, I want you to sell it. Let's have a little of it." [4]

Covering sales territory for Stagg on the east coast during the second half of 1891, Mills typified the salesman whose success was based in great part on personality and his knowledge of distilleries "from the roof down."

The Leestown distilleries were among the first to bottle their whiskeys rather than simply sell them by the barrel. Before the 1880s, Carlisle and O.F.C. had joined W.A. Gaines' Old Crow in bottling their own products. Within a few years of acquiring the Leestown distilleries, George Stagg set up an auxiliary company named Stagg, Hume & Co. to bottle and distribute its whiskeys. Though the firm's office was in St. Louis, the packaging was done in Leestown. O.F.C. was contained in large, distinctive white flint bottles. Blown into the glass was the message "Bottled only at Frankfort, Ky., by Stagg, Hume & Co., sole agents for the distiller." The bottles were then packed in wooden cases, a dozen to the case, and secured with a wire seal. Distinctive bottling and labels afforded distillers some protection from counterfeiters, who were capable of filling common bottles with cheap blended whiskeys, slapping on a look-alike label, and marketing the whiskey at the prices of the established brand.

And imitators there were. In 1882 the Kentucky Distilling Co. of Louisville marketed an inferior-tasting whiskey under the Carlisle name. Alerted by customers, E.H. Taylor, Jr., took the culprits to court and succeeded in curbing the fraud. Taking pride in the pristine quality of its ingredients, the Leestown distilleries distributed circulars attesting to the purity of its spring water as well as the finished whiskey. Nothing so riled Taylor and his fellow producers of straight bourbon whiskey as "a debasement of their brands by association with substandard…or blended whiskey." [5]

One of the greatest issues in bourbon-making toward the end of the century was purity versus adulteration, a distiller's practice that was as old as whiskey making. Taylor and his associates staunchly defended the "purity" of whiskey against adulteration with additives. To improve the flavor or the looks of whiskey, some distillers blended in fruit syrups or other sweeteners as well as other flavorings. In some instances they re-distilled their product or "rectified" it. Most of these additives were benign, but some were hazardous to a drinker's health.

The avowed enemy of these practices, Taylor referred to "neutral spirits, high wines, and alcohol" as the "articles of foreign growth" not native to Kentucky, warning customers against purchasing fake goods. According to his system of values, honorable distillers simply did not blend their whiskey, and low-grade whiskey was never an acceptable substitute for the straight product. In one instance after Taylor's split with the Leestown distilleries, a Louisville rectifier began to sell a rectified whiskey called *Kentucky Taylor.* At the time there was no truth-in-packaging requirement nor was there much protection against infringement. In the court proceedings initiated to protect his name, Taylor contended that he didn't want his brand, *Old Taylor,* confused with a blended whiskey. Fortunately, after about 1890 the George T. Stagg Company does not appear to have had to defend itself against such challenges to its integrity.

One major gain for the Leestown and other distilleries came with the Bottled-in-Bond Act in 1897. This legislation built on the earlier revenue law that required adequate labeling and stamping to distinguish straight whiskey from lesser grades. Under its provisions distillers were allowed to bottle whiskey while it was still in bond, that is, prior to paying a revenue tax on it. When the bottled goods were withdrawn for sale, the distiller paid tax on the fractional amount of whiskey in each bottle — a substantial windfall for the distillery. The green government stamp which was affixed to each bottle certified that the whiskey was at least four years old, that it was 100 proof, and that it was produced during a single season at a single distillery. This served to distinguish so-called straight whiskeys from those that sometimes masqueraded as straight whiskeys when actually they were diluted, rectified, or blended. The result was to hamper the efforts of counterfeiters and vendors of lesser whiskeys from deceiving unsuspecting buyers. Bonded whiskeys safeguarded the consumer from buying those beverages that resembled the "real thing" but were in fact adulterated. In addition to its green stamp, each bottle contained the date of distillation, the distiller's name, and the state of manufacture.

As might be expected, E. H. Taylor, Jr., was a staunch advocate for the bill, pointing out the abuses that often occurred before its enactment:

Under the old act a man can call himself a distiller. He can take a barrel of neutral spirits, warm from the still, and add to it a little essential oil, a little flavoring matter, and a little coloring matter, and if his conscience is especially tender a spoonful or two of real whiskey. He calls this product eight-year old whiskey and sells it to the unsuspecting public as such. He has a product which looks, tastes, smells, and analyzes like real whiskey, but which has a very different effect on the human nervous system.

Ever the defender of the pure product, he goes on to extol the time-tried virtues of making whiskey the old way: No one has yet discovered how to produce a pure and more healthful whiskey, except by aging it, and the green government stamp is simply a form of protection to the honest distiller, who makes his goods by honest process which take eight years to complete, while the compounder turns his out in eight minutes.[6]

The bill represented a setback for the rectifiers and wholesalers who had accumulated profits by selling compounded liquors. They were denied the stamp and thus lacked the government's guarantee of a bottle's contents representing "the real article." In colorful language, Taylor issued one of the most memorable statements in a debate that he was soon to win:

It is an admitted axiom that quality recedes as cheapness advances… the ancient Bourbon flavor has departed and the stomach groans under the dominion of a new ruler."[7]

When the Bottled-in-Bond Act of 1897 passed with the help of John G. Carlisle, a U.S. congressman from Kentucky who would become Treasury Secretary during President Cleveland's second term, Taylor was elated. The act provided that whiskey must be aged for a minimum of four years in warehouses supervised by the federal agents. To qualify as bonded whiskey, it had to be distilled at one place at one time, had to be at least 100 proof (50% alcohol), and its actual maker identified on label. A green label, containing a portrait of John Carlisle as Secretary of the Treasury, was added a decade or so later to honor the secretary for his efforts. Violation of any of the law's provisions was regarded as a serious federal crime. Taylor and the distillers of straight whiskey had scored a victory against those who feigned the real thing and sold it at considerably less than the genuine product cost to produce.

In many respects the life of E. H. Taylor, Jr., mirrors the fortunes of the whiskey industry from the end of the Civil War well into the twentieth century — its ups and downs, its innovations and marketing efforts that eventually lead to its becoming America's preferred and genuinely native alcoholic beverage. Throughout his later distilling career, both at Leestown and Glenn's Creek, Taylor spent much of his energy maintaining or expanding the market for straight whiskey in the face of the encroaching competition of blended whiskey that was cheaper and more abundant. In addition to supervising the operations of his own distillery, he was a tireless promoter and relentless defender of straight whiskey. The whole industry, especially his fellow distillers, benefited greatly from his campaign in their behalf. This was a clear instance of private industry shaping public policy for both its own and the country's benefit.

During the several years of debates and hearings that preceded passage of the Pure Food and Drug Act of 1906, his voice was even more influential in promoting the cause of straight whiskey. Identified with President Theodore Roosevelt's reformist initiatives, the legislation established labeling standards for virtually all food and drug products.

Taylor's efforts had begun as early 1889, when he urged the Kentucky Distillers Association to enact a labeling law. His intent then was to require the producers of "new process" whiskey to acknowledge their efforts to speed up natural processes in order to artificially age and color whiskey. "New process" referred to subjecting whiskey in the barrel to hot air blasts and other "forced" processes.

Accuracy in labeling to prevent fraud and protect consumers was a novel proposal in the late 1880s. His ideas were clearly ahead of his time, since serious discussion of pure food and drug initiatives on a national

level did not begin until 1903.[8] For obvious reasons, the interests of blended whiskeys strenuously resisted his efforts to require accurate labeling and
attacked the proposal in every forum — at trade meetings, before congres-
sional committees, and at national pure food congresses. Taylor contended
that rectified whiskey committed a fraud on the consumer because its producers sold it at rates equivalent to those of straight whiskey, which cost
considerably more time and greater expense to produce. Whatever side one
took on the issue of clear, honest, and adequate labeling, whiskey was, from
the beginning, at the center of the debate.

The battle between proponents of straight whiskey and those representing rectified whiskey became personal as Taylor and Oscar Pepper and
their associates were described as bourbon aristocrats identified with horse
farms, breeders of fancy cattle, and sartorial elegance. Taylor, given the
opportunity, would probably have acknowledged each descriptor as a
compliment, a badge of honor. His farm was celebrated for his prized
Herefords, and he was widely known as a fastidious dresser. The *Louisville
Courier-Journal* on at least one occasion noted in detail what he was wearing —"a faultless frock suit of autumn brown with a bow tie to match."[9]

Though the pure food and drugs law did not specifically mention
whiskey, most Kentucky distillers regarded its passage as a validation of
the "pure" product in which they took so much pride. When it was finally
enacted, they felt vindicated because the law prohibited interstate commerce in "adulterated" or "misbranded" goods. In their view, it was the
safeguard that would distinguish their product from what they perceived
as the adulterations and outright fraud of rectified whiskeys. Cincinnati
rectifiers and compounders, for example, would be liable to prosecution
if they labeled their product "bourbon whiskey." "Whiskey" implied that
the beverage was a distillate of grain. "Bourbon" suggested a product of
mostly corn. When opponents protested application of the law, the issue
was referred to President Roosevelt, who came down in favor of the straight
whiskey interests. Working through the solicitor general, Roosevelt
required that straight whiskey be labeled as "straight whiskey" and that
whiskey produced by mixing two or more straight whiskeys be labeled as

"blended whiskey." A whiskey that contained no actual whiskey but neutral spirits, coloring, and flavoring was to be labeled "imitation whiskey." [10]

The effect of these requirements was to increase the demand and consumption of straight whiskey. Between 1898 and 1903, the average output of bonded whiskey did not exceed 500,000 gallons annually. In response to increased demand, after 1903 the output of bonded whiskey increased to 700,000 gallons, then to one million to 1.5 million within the next two years. [11] In effect, the Pure Food and Drug Act had largely resolved the problem of counterfeit whiskey.

During the ensuing decades the distilleries at Leestown under the George T. Stagg Company and others were to undergo changes as the industry evolved, often prospering and sometimes struggling, through two world wars. In the new century, new leadership came from a family long associated with the Leestown distilleries. Albert Bacon Blanton presided over the Stagg Distillery at Leestown through the early decades of the twentieth century. The Blanton name was almost as old as Leestown itself, and generations of Blantons had been associated with the Leestown distilleries almost from the beginning.

In 1897, at sixteen years of age, Albert Bacon Blanton hired on as an office boy at the George T. Stagg distillery, beginning a career in whiskey at Leestown that was to last fifty-five years. Within a year the industrious young man had been promoted to a clerical job. A quick study, he took a four-month course to improve his skills in typing and shorthand. By choice he asked to work in each department, eventually over the next few years performing nearly every job at the distillery.

Before he was twenty, he was appointed superintendent of the distillery, its warehouses, and the bottling shop where previously he had corked hand-filled bottles. Elected to the executive board of Stagg distillery in 1909, he became plant manager in 1912. The New York owners, recognizing that he was indispensable, made him president of George T. Stagg Co. in 1921; in 1929 he negotiated the contract under which Schenley Products Company of New York purchased the distillery and kept it open during the Prohibition years with the production of medicinal whiskey — the only

Kentucky company to do so. Under his leadership the distillery survived during those dark, dry years into the period of recovery under the ownership of Schenley Distillers, a company later characterizing Blanton as the "Dean of America's Bourbon distillers." Like his predecessor E. H. Taylor, Jr., he was wedded to the production of straight Kentucky bourbon and regarded compounds and blends as inferior to the "real thing." For the remainder of his long career he continued as manager and master distiller, recognized as much for his vast stock of whiskey lore as for his savvy in all phases of producing a quality product.

Under his direction the physical plant at Leestown underwent significant advances. In addition to new buildings that give the distillery much the appearance it has today, he built a landmark stone residence on Stony Point above the distillery grounds overlooking Wilkinson Boulevard. Marrying in 1934, he designed and oversaw construction of the house with great attention. When it was completed, the home was used for entertaining as well as a home for his family. During those evenings, he served what was his favorite bourbon — that aged in Warehouse H — the same warehouse in which the river rose four feet above the first-floor elevation during the 1937 flood. It is a tribute to Blanton and his employees that within twenty-four hours of the water's receding from the plant site, the Stagg distillery was back in full operation. "Stony Point," which served during his long tenure as his family's home, now houses administrative offices for the Buffalo Trace Distillery.

Bearing the honorific title of "Colonel" (as with E. H. Taylor, Jr., selected by the state governor as a Kentucky Colonel), Albert Blanton drew on the expertise of famed local architect Leo L. Oberwarth to design the terraced gardens and flower beds at the heart of the distillery, creating a kind of park which is now adjacent to the distillery clubhouse. The Elmer T. Lee Clubhouse, still used for meetings and receptions as well as a dining area for the distillery's employees, was constructed from four log houses that were disassembled and recycled into the handsome structure seen today. Its huge fieldstone fireplaces and wrap-around verandah, flanked with rough wood balustrades, give the log building a peaceful, rustic air in keeping with the long history of the distillery and surrounding community of Leestown. Among the other buildings Blanton constructed on the landscaped grounds are a cockhouse (for the Colonel's fighting cocks) and a burgoo house containing two ninety-gallon iron kettles, a wood-burning oven for bread, and a built-in barbecue pit used on social occasions in the best traditions of old Kentucky. This beautiful park-like area at the center of the distillery commemorates Leestown as it was, the setting for a sylvan spring at which herds of buffalo watered, an area of great natural beauty. Following in the tradition of Oscar Pepper and E. H. Taylor, Jr., Albert Bacon Blanton was a bourbon aristocrat, a master who took as much pride in the environment in which whiskey was made as he did in the final product.

His long life at the distillery paralleled the key events of his century — the lean years of Prohibition under the Eighteenth Admendment (1920-1933), which put all but a few of Kentucky's distilleries out of business; the Great Depression; the era when organized crime entered into bootlegging; the flood of 1937, which inundated the distillery grounds; the war years when the plant produced only straight alcohol for military purposes; and the increasingly complex modern era in which a steady proliferation of laws regulate the production and sale of whiskey. From these trials and challenges it has survived and prospered, one of only a few of the two hundred distilleries operating before Prohibition that has prospered after repeal.

Under Albert Blanton's guidance the company underwent significant expansion as sales increased and new brands were introduced. One of them, "Cove Spring," evoked memories of the pure-water spring that the first surveyors encountered as they camped at Leestown, the source on which generations of distillers drew to produce whiskeys that equaled any, and surpassed most, produced in Kentucky and beyond.

Since 1869 a continuously operating distillery has occupied the site of Leestown, whose history reaches back to Kentucky's infancy and looks ahead to its productive future. By 1933 when the Twenty-first Amendment repealed Prohibition, the George T. Stagg distillery of Leestown was one of six surviving, operational distilleries in Kentucky. Recognized as one of the preeminent producers of straight whiskey, in 1939 the distillery entered a golden era when Ancient Age, four years of age and 90 proof, was introduced to the market. Between 1937 and 1939, the Leestown plant distilled or bottled more than thirty brands of Schenley whiskey, including such brand names as "Henry Clay," "James E. Pepper," "T. W. Samuels," and "Buffalo Springs." During 1935 the Schenley distillery straight bourbon "Cream of Kentucky" was among the best selling whiskeys, as was "Old Quaker," its straight rye whiskey. Among rye blends, "Golden Wedding" held a substantial portion of the market. The robustness of the company's sales was halted only by the cataclysmic immersion of the country in World War II when virtually every segment of the economy was transformed and mobilized to challenge the aggression of the Axis powers.

During the war years the Leestown distillery joined a nationwide movement to support the war effort. By the fall of 1942 production of whiskey was halted by the War Production Board, which proscribed that the nation's distilleries convert to produce straight alcohol for the war effort. This distillery was allowed to produce whiskey every other month. Leestown bottom is entering its third century as a site for the production of fine whiskey. It was not until 1982 that Schenley sold its Ancient Age distillery at Leestown to Ancient Age Distilling Company, a newly formed New York company. Among its accomplishments was the development of the Blanton brand, a single-barrel bourbon named for Albert Bacon Blanton, the distiller and manager most identified with the company during the twentieth century. In reviving yet another name long associated with the industry and Leestown, Ancient Age drew on the site's long and distinguished tradition of whiskey-making. Growing out of Albert Blanton's personal taste for single-barrel bourbon, the Leestown distillery was first to market a single-barrel whiskey.

Ancient Age owned the Leestown distillery until September 30, 1992, when the Leestown Company, a subsidiary of the Sazerac Company of New Orleans, purchased it. The name was changed to Buffalo Trace Distillery in June 1999. Immediately its new owners undertook major renovations and beautification as a matter of company pride as well as a means to promote Buffalo Trace, its new flagship bourbon.

In large part, the history of the distilleries at Leestown, through many incarnations and brand names, is the history of the evolution of bourbon in Kentucky — from the raw products of early settlement to the refined and premium whiskeys produced there for nearly two centuries. Drawing in part on early innovations made along neighboring Glenn's Creek, Leestown has been a major center of development in the whiskey industry, especially through the major influence of E. H. Taylor, Jr., who had associations with distillers and distilleries at both sites. The first distillery to incorporate the use of steam power, the first to use climate-controlled warehousing, the first to market single-barrel bourbon to satisfy the most discriminating tastes, the bourbon-makers along the banks of the Kentucky River at Leestown have been pioneers and innovators, never losing sight of the traditions that have brought their whiskeys over two centuries to eminence in the industry.

Since Buffalo Trace has assumed ownership, the grounds have been landscaped to provide an idyllic setting in which to preserve the traditions of whiskey-making at its best. The site offers a pastoral atmosphere to the thousands of tourists who come to visit the distillery each year as well as those who come to work at its facilities each day. In early 2001 *Malt Advocate Magazine* named Buffalo Trace its "Distillery of the Year," a prestigious international award never before given to an American distillery, having been bestowed only on distilleries in Scotland and Ireland. John Hansell, publisher of the magazine, said, "I've seen more progress in one year at Buffalo Trace than I've seen in an entire decade at some other distilleries." The company also has made an effective outreach to the Frankfort community, serving as a major sponsor of events like the Kentucky Folklife Festival held on the grounds of the Old State Capitol. Justifiably proud of its past, the company seeks to educate discriminating consumers about a product that originated in Kentucky and that dates from earliest settlement at the important bend in the Kentucky River where buffalo crossed the waters to forage their way through the hills and "pleasant level" of what was to become the nation's fifteenth state.

Notes

I. *"A Richer and More Beautiful Country"*

1. Nicholas Cresswell, *The Journal of Nicholas Cresswell, 1774-1777,* The Dial Press, New York, 1924, p. 78.

2. Ibid., pp. 78-79.

3. Ibid., p. 80.

4. James Nourse, "Journey to Kentucky in 1775," *The Journal of American History,* Vol. 19, Nos. 2,3, and 4, New York, 1925.

5. Archer Butler Hulbert, *Paths of the Mound-Building Indians and Great Game Animals,* Historic Highways of America, Vol. 1, Frontier Press, Inc., Cleveland, Ohio, 1967, p. 119.

6. The Journal of Christopher Gist in Willard Rouse Jillson's *Early Frankfort and Franklin County,* The Standard Printing Company, Louisville, Ky., 1936, p. 8.

7. Samuel Wilson, "Leestown — Its Founders and History," *Register of the Kentucky Historical Society,* Vol. 29, No. 89, Frankfort, Ky., October, 1931, p. 386.

8. Ibid.

9. Ibid., p. 391.

10. Robert McAfee, The McAfee Journals, in Willard Rouse Jillson's *Early Frankfort and Franklin County,* p. 12.

11. James McAfee, The McAfee Journals, in Jillson's *Early Frankfort and Franklin County,* p. 11-12.

12. Neal Hammon, "Historic Lawsuits of the Eighteenth Century Locating "The Stamping Grounds," *Register of the Kentucky Historical Society,* Vol. 79, No. 3, July 1971, pp. 204-205.

13. Nourse, Entry for 30 May 1775.

14. Cresswell, pp. 80-81.

15. Ibid., pp. 84-85.

16. Ibid., p. 85.

17. Ibid.

18. Wilson, p. 392.

19. Mary B. Kegley, *Early Adventures on the Western Waters,* Vol. 2, Green Publishers, Inc., Orange, Virginia, Virginia, 1982, pp. 14-15.

20. Ibid.

21. Richard Henderson, "The Journal of Richard Henderson." Draper Ms.

22. Humphrey Marshall, *The History of Kentucky*, Vol. 1, Frankfort, Ky., printed by Henry Gore, 1812, pp. 25-26.

23. John Floyd, Letter to George Rogers Clark, 16 April 1781, in *The Letters of John Floyd*, Neal Hammon and Nelson Dawson, eds., (Unpublished, Filson Club).

24. Mary Verhoeff, *The Kentucky River Navigation*, Filson Club Publications, John P. Morton and Company, 1917, p. 77.

25. Ibid., p. 77.

26. Cresswell, p. 85.

27. Jillson, *Early Frankfort and Franklin County*, p.37.

28. Ibid.

29. Reuben Gold Thwaites and Louise Phelps Kellogg, *The Revolution on the Upper Ohio, 1775-1777* (first published 1908), Kennikat Press, Port Washington, 1970, pp. 175-176.

30. John Floyd, Unpublished letter to William Preston, 21 July 1776.

31. John Floyd, Unpublished letter to William Preston, 21 May 1776.

32. Levi Todd, "General Levi Todd's Narrative," in Willard Rouse Jillson's *Tales of the Dark and Bloody Ground*, C.T. Dearing Printing Company, Louisville, Ky., 1930, p. 72.

33. Lewis Collins, *History of Kentucky*, (revised by Richard Collins), Vol. 2, (originally published in 1874 and reprinted in 1976), Kentucky Imprints, Berea, Ky., p. 242.

34. Willard Rouse Jillson, *Sketches of Early Frankfort*, Roberts Printing Company, Frankfort, Ky., 1967, p. 12.

35. Jillson, *Early Frankfort and Franklin County*, p. 40.

36. Verhoeff, p. 35.

37. Jillson, *The Kentucky Country*, Washington, D.C.: H.L. & J.B. McQueen, Inc., 1931, p. 35.

38. A Resident of Frankfort, "The Kentucky River and Its Islands," *Register of the Kentucky Historical Society*, Vol. 1, 1903, p. 41.

39. *Biographical Cyclopedia of the Commonwealth of Kentucky*, J.M Gresham Company, Chicago, Philadelphia, 1898, p. 393.

40. Charles Parrish, "Navigation Development on the Kentucky River," *The Army Engineer*, Vol. 3, No. 1, Army Engineer Association, March/April, 1995, p. 19.

41. Mary Taylor Brewer, *From Log Cabins to the White House: A History of the Taylor Family*, Mary Taylor Brewer (publisher), Wooton, Ky., 1985, p. 335.

II. *Antebellum Leestown*

1. Mary Willis Woodson, "History of the Lee Family," in *Through the Portals of Glen Willis,* Franklin County Trust for Historic Preservation, (no date), Frankfort, Ky., p. 6.

2. Ibid.

3. Interview with Alice Blanton, Frankfort, Ky.

4. Annie Pierce Steger, "River 'Rope Walks' Supplied Riverboats, Ocean Vessels," *Frankfort State Journal,* Article No. 4, October 13, 1965, p. 11.

5. Mary Willis Woodson, "My Recollections of Frankfort," in *Through the Portals of Glen Willis,* p. 13.

6. Verhoeff, p. 93.

7. J. Winston Coleman, Jr., "Kentucky River Steamboats," *Register of the Kentucky Historical Society,* Vol. 63, October, 1965, p. 300.

8. J. Winston Coleman, Jr., *Steamboats on the Kentucky,* Winburn Farm, Lexington, Ky., 1960, p. 6.

9. Ebenezer Stedman, *Bluegrass Craftsman,* edited by Frances L. S. Dugan and Jacqueline P. Bull, University of Kentucky Press, Lexington, Ky., 1959, p. 132.

III. *Leestown Distilling: The Early Years*

1. John Ed. Pearce, *Nothing Better in the Bluegrass,* Brown-Forman Distilling Corporation, (n.d.), p. 15.

2. Museum display note, Hopewell Museum, Paris, Kentucky.

3. Bruce Algar, "The Bourbon Dynasty," *Louisville Magazine,* April 1992, p.79.

4. Ibid.

5. Carl Kramer, *Capital on the Kentucky,* Historic Frankfort, Inc., Frankfort, Ky., 1986, p. 56.

6. Ibid., pp. 56-57.

7. Jillson, *Early Frankfort and Franklin County,* p. 129.

8. Algar, p. 79.

9. D. G. Churchill, *The Whiskey History of Leestown, Kentucky,* 1769-1982, (Unpublished Ms., Buffalo Trace Distillery), p. 24.

10. William E. Ellis, *The Kentucky River,* University Press of Kentucky, Lexington, Ky., 2000, p. 11.

11. Coleman, "Kentucky River Steamboats," p. 302.

12. Churchill, p. 25.

IV. *Whiskey Comes of Age*

1. L. F. Johnson, *The History of Franklin County*, Roberts Printing Company, Frankfort, Ky., 1912, p. 152.

2. Kramer, pp. 168-169.

3. Ibid., p. 197.

4. Johnson, pp. 269-270.

5. Family Scrapbook of E. H. Taylor, Jr. (Library of John Hay, Frankfort, Ky.)

6. Temple Bodley, Samuel Wilson, et. al., *History of Kentucky*, Vol. 4, The S.J. Clarke Publishing Company, Louisville, Ky., 1928, p. 863.

7. Gerald Alvey, *Kentucky Bluegrass Country*, University Press of Mississippi, Jackson and London, 1992, p. 237.

8. Churchill, p. 34.

9. Ibid., p. 35.

10. Ibid., p. 36.

11. National Association of Blenders, Rectifiers, and Rectifying Distillers, *The Fable of the Arab and the Beggar*, (n.p.), 1908, pp. 4-9.

12. Churchill, p. 37.

13. *Frankfort State Journal*, October 9, 1978.

14. Churchill, p. 38.

15. Ibid., p. 45.

16. Ibid., p. 47.

17. Ibid., p. 49.

18. Ibid.

19. Ibid., p. 55.

20. Ibid., p. 57.

21. Charles D. Hockensmith, *A Study of Bricks from the Kentucky River Mills Site, Frankfort, Franklin County*, Kentucky, Kentucky Heritage Council, Frankfort, Ky, June 1998.

22. Churchill, p. 59.

23. Ibid., p. 60.

24. Ibid., p. 61.

25. Ibid.

V. *The Pure Product and its Producer*

1. Churchill, p. 101.

2. Ibid.

3. Ibid., p. 103.

4. Ibid., p. 102.

5. Ibid., p. 103.

6. E. H. Taylor, Jr., "The Rule of the Regions: An Essay on Distilling in Kentucky," Frankfort, Ky., 1908, p. 4.

7. Churchill, p. 101.

8. Ibid., p. 104.

9. Ibid., p. 106.

10. Ibid., p. 107.

11. Interview with Mrs. V. O. Barnard, Frankfort, Ky.

12. Charles Kendrick Cowdery, *The Bourbon Country Reader,* Vol. 4, Number 6, October 1999, p. 2.

13. Gerald Carson, *The Social History of Bourbon,* Dodd, Mead Publishers, New York, 1963, p.87.

14. George T. Stagg pamphlet, Leestown distilleries, promoting O.F.C. whiskey.

15. Davis Lee Jahncke, Jr., Ancient Age Distillery, Frankfort, Kentucky, *Existing Buildings Analysis* (New Orleans, Jahncke Architects, Inc.), 1993, entries for buildings 101, 102, 103.

16. Churchill, p. 63.

17. Ibid., p. 64.

18. Ibid., p. 65.

19. Ibid., p. 144.

20. Ibid., p. 67.

21. Ibid., p. 71.

22. Ibid., p. 74.

23. Interview with E. H. Taylor Hay, Jr., Frankfort, Ky.

24. Ibid.

VI. *Toward the New Century*

1. Churchill, p. 74.

2. Ibid., p. 76.

3. Ibid., p. 78.

4. *Wine and Spirit Bulletin,* vol. 5, no. 12, June 18, 1891, pp. 19-20.

5. Churchill, p. 124.

6. *New York Times,* October 16, 1904, p. 7.

7. Cowdery, "Remembering the Father of the Modern Bourbon Industry," *The Bourbon Country Reader,* Vol. 4, No. 6, p. 3.

8. Churchill, p. 125.

9. *The Courier-Journal,* September 2, 1902, p. 9.

10. Churchill, p. 129.

11. *New York Times,* April 12, 1907, p. 3.

Selected Bibliography

Alvey, Gerald. *Kentucky Bluegrass Country.* Jackson and London: University Press of Mississippi, 1992.

Biographical Cyclopedia of the Commonwealth of Kentucky. Chicago, Philadelphia: J.M. Gresham Company, 1896.

Brewer, Mary Taylor. *From Log Cabins to the White House: A History of the Taylor Family.* Wooton, Ky.: Mary Taylor Brewer (publisher), 1985.

Carson, Gerald. *The Social History of Bourbon.* New York: Dodd, Mead Publishers, 1963.

Chinn, George Morton. *Kentucky: Settlement and Statehood, 1750-1800.* Frankfort, Ky.: Kentucky Historical Society, 1975.

Churchill, D. G. *Ancient Age through the Ages: The Whiskey History of Leestown, Kentucky, 1769-1982.* (Unpublished, Buffalo Trace Distillery)

Coleman, J. Winston, Jr. "Steamboats on the Kentucky." *Register of the Kentucky Historical Society,* Vol. 63, No. 4, October 1965, pp. 299-322.

______. *Steamboats on the Kentucky River.* Lexington, Ky.: Winburn Press, 1960.

Collins, Richard and Lewis. Berea, Ky.: *History of Kentucky,* 2 vols., [1874] reprinted by Kentucky Imprints, 1976.

Cresswell, Nicholas. *The Journal of Nicholas Cresswell, 1774-1777.* New York: The Dial Press, 1924.

Darlington, William M. *Christopher Gist's Journals.* Pittsburgh: J.R. Weldon and Co., 1893.

Dugan, Frances L. S., and Jacqueline P. Bull, eds. *Bluegrass Craftsman.* Lexington, Ky.: University of Kentucky Press, 1959.

Ellis, William E. *The Kentucky River,* Lexington, Ky.: The University Press of Kentucky, 2000.

Glenn, Nettie Henry. *Early Frankfort Kentucky 1786-1861.* Frankfort, Ky., 1986.

Hammon, Neal. "Historic Law Suits of the Eighteenth Century." *Register of the Kentucky Historical Society,* Vol. 69, No. 3, July 1974, pp. 197-215.

Hammon, Neal, and Nelson Dawson, eds. *The Letters of John Floyd:1774-1783,* (Unpublished, Filson Club)

Hinds, Charles. "The Pioneers," *Franklin County 1795-1995*. Frankfort, Ky.: Frankfort State Journal, Franklin County Bicentennial Edition, May 7, 1995.

Hockensmith, Charles D. *A Study of Bricks from the Kentucky River Mills Site.* Frankfort, Ky.: Kentucky Heritage Commission, Frankfort, 1998.

Hulbert, Archer Butler. *Paths of the Mound-Building Indians and Great Game Animals.* Historic Highways of America, Vol.1. Cleveland, Ohio: Frontier Press, 1967.

Hughes, Nicky. "Fort Boone and the Civil War Defense of Frankfort." *Register of the Kentucky Historical Society,* Vol. 88, No. 2, Spring 1990, pp. 148-162.

Jillson, Willard Rouse. *Early Frankfort and Franklin County.* Louisville, Ky.: The Standard Printing Company, 1936.

______. *Tales of the Dark and Bloody Ground.* Louisville, Ky.: C.T. Dearing Printing Company, 1930.

______. *The First Landowners of Frankfort, Kentucky 1774-1790.* Frankfort, Ky: The State Journal, 1945.

______. *The Kentucky Country.* Washington, D.C.: H.L. & J.B. McQueen, Inc., 1931, [Reprinting in facsimile, *The Kentucky Countrie: The Discovery, Purchase, and Settlement of the Country of Kentuckie in North America* by Alexander Fitzroy, London, 1786].

______. *Sketches of Early Frankfort.* Frankfort, Ky.: Roberts Printing Company, 1967.

Johnson, L. F. *The History of Franklin County, Ky.* Frankfort, Ky.: Roberts Printing Company, 1912.

Kegley, Mary B. *Early Adventures on the Western Waters.* 2 vols., Orange, Va.: Green Publishers, Inc., 1982.

Kramer, Carl. *Capital on the Kentucky, A Two Hundred Year History of Frankfort & Franklin County.* Frankfort. Ky.: Historic Frankfort, Inc., 1986.

McAfee, James and Roberts. "The McAfee Journals" in *The Woods-McAfee Memorial, Neander Woods.* Louisville, Ky.: Courier-Journal Job Printing Co., 1905, pp. 424-453.

Marshall, Humphrey. *The History of Kentucky,* Frankfort, Ky.: Henry Gore, 1812.

Nourse, James. "Journey to Kentucky in 1775," *Journal of American History,* Volume 19, Nos. 2,3,4, 1925.

Parrish, Charles. "History of Navigation on the Kentucky River," *The Army Engineer,* Vol. 3, No. 1, Army Engineer Association, March/April 1995, pp. 17-20.

Pearce, John Ed. *Nothing Better in the Bluegrass*. Louisville, Ky.: Brown Foreman
 Distilling Corporation, (n.d.).

Taylor, E.H., Jr. *The Rule of the Regions: An Essay on Distilling in Kentucky,*
 Frankfort, Ky.: Frankfort Printing Co., 1908.

______. Taylor Family Scrapbook (in the possession of John Hay), Frankfort,
 Kentucky.

Thwaites, Reuben, and Louise Phelps Kellogg. *The Revolution on the Upper Ohio,
 1775-1777.* Port Washington, New York: Kennikat Press, 1908 (reprinted 1970.)

Verhoeff, Mary. *The Kentucky River Navigation.* Louisville, Ky.: Filson Club
 Publications, Number 28, J.P. Morton & Company, 1917.

Wilson, Samuel. "Leestown — Its Founders and History," *Register of the Kentucky
 Historical Society,* Vol. 29, No 89, October, 1931, pp. 385-396.

Woodson, Mary Willis. "My Recollections of Frankfort," in *Through the Portals of
 Glen Willis.* Compiled by Martha Moore. Frankfort, Ky.: Franklin County
 Trust for Historic Preservation, [n.d.].

Family Tree of Taylors Associated with Leestown

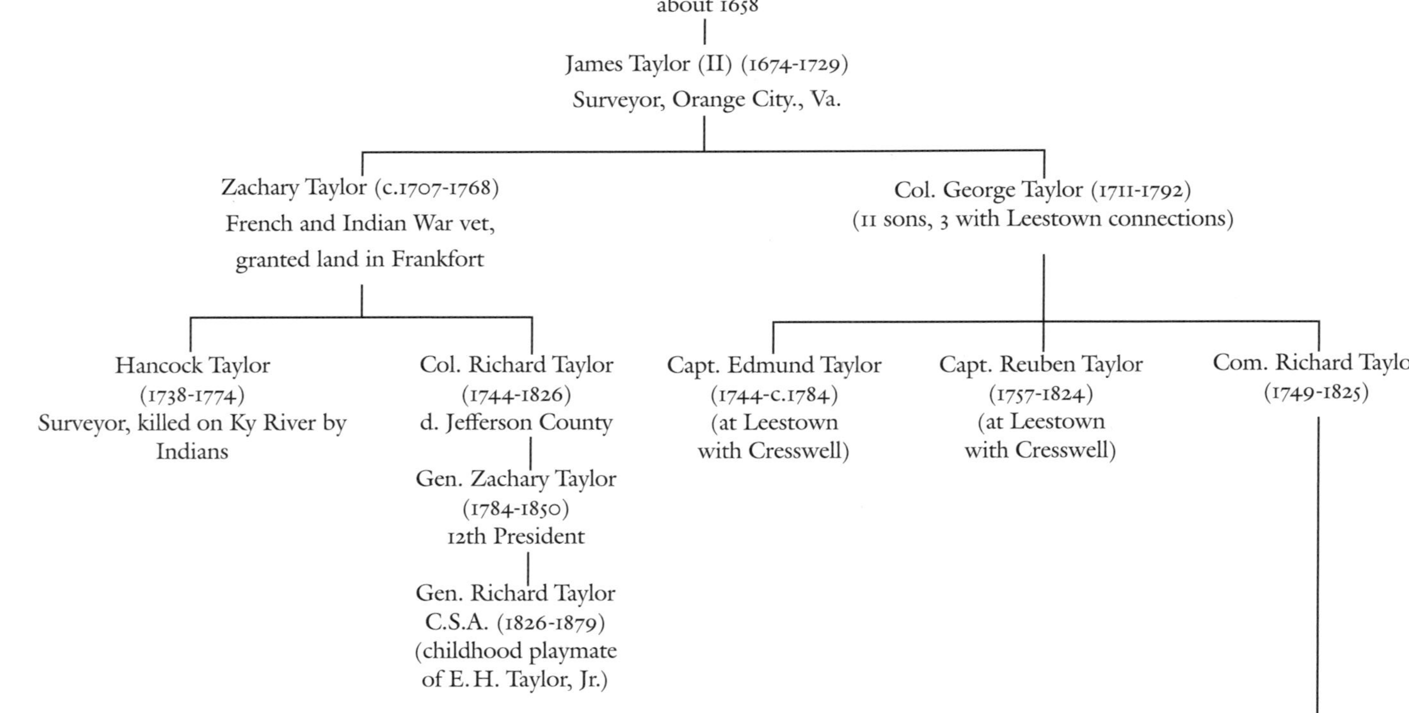

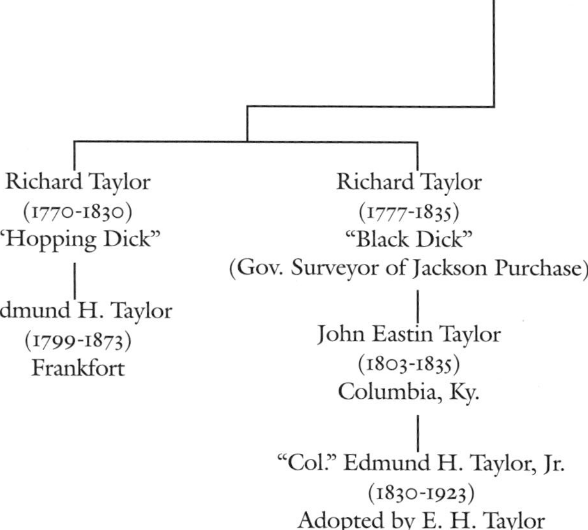

Richard Taylor
(1770-1830)
"Hopping Dick"

Edmund H. Taylor
(1799-1873)
Frankfort

Richard Taylor
(1777-1835)
"Black Dick"
(Gov. Surveyor of Jackson Purchase)

John Eastin Taylor
(1803-1835)
Columbia, Ky.

"Col." Edmund H. Taylor, Jr.
(1830-1923)
Adopted by E. H. Taylor

The text of this book was designed & typeset by Jonathan Greene

using Carter & Cone Galliard and Mantinia typefaces

designed by Matthew Carter. The cover and dustjacket

were designed by Black Sheep, Inc.